COLLEGE LIFE AT OLD OGLETHORPE

CENTRAL HALL OF OGLETHORPE UNIVERSITY

From an old lithograph

COLLEGE LIFE
AT
OLD OGLETHORPE

Allen P. Tankersley

THE UNIVERSITY OF GEORGIA PRESS

ATHENS

Paperback edition, 2009
© 1951 by the University of Georgia Press
Athens, Georgia 30602
www.ugapress.org
Printed digitally in the United States of America

The Library of Congress has cataloged the hardcover edition of this book as follows:
Library of Congress Cataloging-in-Publication Data

Tankersley, Allen P., 1908–1957.
College life at old Oglethorpe.
xiii, 184 p. illus., ports. 24 cm.
Bibliography: p. 171–178.
1. Oglethorpe University, Milledgeville, Ga.—History. I. Title.
LD4191.O462 T3
378.758   51-7218

Paperback ISBN-13: 978-0-8203-3453-0
ISBN-10: 0-8203-3453-7

Cover illustration: Central Hall of Oglethorpe University, from an old lithograph.

To
Thornwell Jacobs
whose unparalleled vision and
devotion to an ideal
refounded
old Oglethorpe University;
and
whose untiring efforts for over thirty years
caused
new Oglethorpe University
to live again
for the service of the South
and
the nation

Preface

OGLETHORPE University, the first chartered denominational school of higher learning in Georgia, was founded by pious Presbyterians who aimed both at "training the minds of the rising generation in the study of useful science" and in imbuing their hearts with the sentiments of religion and virtue. The founders believed that the "cultivation of piety and diffusion of useful knowledge" formed an inseparable twain, and they saw in the union of education and religion the wisdom of the world combining with the revelation of God to bless mankind.[1]

Thus Oglethorpe was born the child of the Church, and Christian teachings were stamped upon it at birth. Its founders were devout Presbyterian ministers and laymen who were willing to work and sacrifice to establish a college in Georgia. Its first faculty—and subsequent ones as well—were all Presbyterians whose godly lives were as impressive as their formal instruction. The students were by and large the sons of men like the founders and professors. Many upon entering Oglethorpe were already professed Christians, and few left the University without the mark of religion indelibly impressed upon them.

The students at Oglethorpe came in contact with a combined religious and intellectual system which completely changed their lives and which sent them forth into the world as ministers, Christian laymen, and leaders in medicine, politics, science, the teaching profession, and other honorable pursuits. As "the child is father to the man," so Oglethorpe was parent to her sons who occupied places of greatest importance in the history of Georgia and the South. The transformation wrought at the University is the story of the life of the students, the professors, the officers, and the townspeople of the college and college community.

---

1. Preface to charter of Oglethorpe University in Oliver H. Prince, *Digest of the Laws of the State of Georgia* (Second edition, Athens, 1837), 877-878.

That story in itself is significant and forms an important chapter in the cultural and intellectual history of the Old South. Yet it has a more basic historical meaning. After 1840 most Georgians who received higher education attended church schools—Oglethorpe, Emory, or Mercer. The religious influence exerted by these colleges permeated through their students to the general population and was felt in every part of the state. By 1861 ministers of the Gospel and other Christian leaders trained in the church colleges of the state were as important in formulating public opinion as were the politicians and the statesmen. At the beginning of the War Between the States, Oglethorpe had graduated two hundred and ninety-four men, including sixty-five ministers, one magazine editor, three or four newspaper editors, several college presidents, a countless number of professors and public school teachers, and the usual quota of lawyers and doctors, besides innumerable planters. At least a thousand had studied in her halls.

The University had had efficient and talented professors. The first president, Dr. Carlisle P. Beman, was one of the leading educators in ante bellum Georgia, and Dr. Samuel K. Talmage was not only an able teacher and college president but also a theologian and religious writer of national influence. Joseph Le Conte, professor of chemical geology and natural history, was one of the foremost American geologists in the nineteenth century. During the same period his successor, Dr. James Woodrow, was the chief spokesman of Southern scientists in their controversy with the theologians. He denied that there is an essential conflict between the Bible and science, and was the first college professor in Georgia to teach the theory of evolution. Sidney Lanier, tutor in ancient languages, 1860-1861, was soon to become a noted literary critic, a distinguished musician, and Georgia's greatest poet.

The influence of such men—students and faculty members—was as incalculable as it was far-reaching, even to the present day.

In portraying college life at old Oglethorpe, I have performed a labor of love. From the age of ten, when I memorized "The Song of the Chattahoochee," I have loved and admired its author, Sidney Lanier. When I grew older and sought to discover the secret of the poet's genius by studying his educational background, I found that Oglethorpe, the only college he ever attended, had had a most eventful and noteworthy history that I thought ought to be recorded.

Once during Reconstruction, in the bitterness of a soul smitten with defeat and despair, Lanier referred to Oglethorpe as "a farcical college," but on maturer reflection he later confessed that he had received some of the most lasting influences of his entire career at that small church school.

The present work is the life story of that college.

ALLEN P. TANKERSLEY

Atlanta, Georgia
December 15, 1950

Acknowledgments

THE research and composition of a work such as the present one necessarily requires the assistance of many persons to the author. The fact that Oglethorpe University was closed for slightly more than forty years and that during this period its records were scattered into various hands, or completely lost, has immeasurably increased the problem of finding source materials upon which to base the history of the school. Except for the help and cooperation of those who found and preserved these scattered sources, no writer could, or would, have undertaken to tell the life story of old Oglethorpe.

To Dr. Thornwell Jacobs, who refounded the University in 1913, I owe a special debt for his collecting as many of the old records as he could. These were deposited in the archives of the new Oglethorpe, and Dr. Philip Weltner, the present head of the University, has given me unrestricted access to them.

Mrs. Leola Beeson found the Minutes of the Thalian Literary Society, 1859-1863, and deposited them in the Georgia State College for Women in Milledgeville. These Minutes were generously made available to me by Mrs. Beeson and the staff of the Library.

Miss Pauline McKinley, of Milledgeville, has preserved the Minutes of the Executive Committee and allowed me to use them to advantage. She also let me use many other items listed in my bibliography.

To Dr. E. Merton Coulter, professor of history at the University of Georgia, I am especially grateful. His *College Life in the Old South* has served both as a model and an inspiration in the preparation of this book. Dr. Coulter informed me of valuable source materials, particularly the George S. Barnsley Papers in the University of North Carolina Library, which inspired my Chapter V on "Religion and Science." He also read my manuscript and made valuable suggestions, which proved profitable.

Others at the University of Georgia who read my manuscript in part or entirely were: Dr. Tomlinson Fort, head of the mathematics department; Dean R. P. Brooks, professor emeritus of business administration; Dean John E. Drewry, head of the Henry W. Grady School of Journalism; Mr. Wimberly W. DeRenne, archivist; and Mr. Ralph Stephens, director of the University Press. To each of them I wish to express my debt of gratitude for the many valuable criticisms offered while this book was being prepared.

I owe a similar debt to Dr. Fletcher M. Green, professor of history at the University of North Carolina, who advised me repeatedly from the time when I first began my research on Oglethorpe in 1946.

To name individually all the others from whom I have received assistance would be a hopeless task, for the list is so long that some surely would be omitted; but I shall conclude by thanking Dr. Philip Weltner, who first suggested the book and who encouraged the work to its completion.

Contents

Illustrations

COLLEGE LIFE AT OLD OGLETHORPE

CHAPTER I

A University on a Hill

ON Wednesday, October 21, 1835, a small group of pious Presbyterians assembled in the Masonic Hall at Milledgeville, Georgia, to consider the very important matter of founding a college. There were only eight present—four laymen and four ministers—but Hopewell Presbytery had appointed a total of twenty-four men to serve on the committee.[1] Doubtless the absentees did not realize the importance of the business that they had been commissioned to do, for at that time there was not a church college of liberal arts in all that vast expanse of territory between the Atlantic and the Pacific and south of Virginia to the Gulf of Mexico.

By the 1830's Georgia was fast developing interest in religious education, and several denominations were beginning to vie with one another in this field, but at the beginning of the century the state, still suffering from the effects of the American Revolution, was woefully lacking both in religion and education. During that struggle Georgia had been almost depopulated in the internecine war between the Whigs and Tories in a horrible carnival of murder and pillage that drove thousands from their homes, killed many more, and closed every church and school within the realm. When peace came, the state was so decimated that its population was less than 75,000, but it was not long until new immigrants began swarming in from the north.

During the Revolution many of "Light Horse Harry" Lee's and Nathanael Greene's soldiers noticed the fertility of Georgia's soil and the beauty of her mountains and valleys, and when the war was over they returned with thousands of their fellows in

---

1. Trustee Minutes of Oglethorpe University, 1835-70, p. 1. These MS minutes are kept in the vault of the present Oglethorpe University in Atlanta. Hereinafter cited as T. Minutes, 1835-70.

such hordes that by 1800 they far outnumbered the older settlers. These newcomers were "the restless, land-hungry, gambling, hard-drinking gentry from as far north as Maryland," who went straight to the frontier and who were fleeing to escape the "hell-fire and brimstone" eruptions of the Jonathan Edwardses that they had left behind them.[2] They cared little either for religion or for schools.

Another group of immigrants, not so large, but far more influential, was made up chiefly of Northerners from New England, New York, Pennsylvania, and New Jersey, who tended to settle in the towns and more thickly populated areas. "They came to be governors, politicians, lawyers, teachers in academies, and managers of whatever needed managing."[3] It was from this group, many of whom were Yale, Middlebury, or Princeton graduates, that leadership came in the educational affairs of early Georgia. Abraham Baldwin, a graduate of Yale and former tutor in his Alma Mater, was one of the first of these immigrants. Giving up the ministry, he came to Georgia near the end of 1783, became a lawyer, and entered politics. His ability was soon recognized, and he was made the first president of the University of Georgia.[4] For the most part the immigrants from New England, like Baldwin, were Congregationalists, but finding few churches of that denomination, they joined the Presbyterian Church and united with the graduates of Princeton in their zeal for education and religion.

When Hopewell Presbytery was set off from the South Carolina Presbytery in 1796, there were less than fifteen Presbyterian churches in Georgia. At that time the field of Hopewell included the whole state, which extended to the Mississippi, and there were only five ministers to serve this vast area. During the twenty-five years after 1796, John Springer, a native of Delaware and graduate of Princeton; Remembrance Chamberlain, a native of Vermont and graduate of Middlebury; Alonzo Church, of the same state and college; Robert Finley, a native of New Jersey and graduate of Princeton; and Nathan S. S. Beman, a New Yorker and graduate of Middlebury, gave Presbyterianism a fresh impetus in Geor-

---

2. E. Merton Coulter, *College Life in the Old South* (New York, 1928), 3, 193. Hereinafter cited as Coulter, *College Life*.
3. *Ibid.*, 3.
4. *Ibid.*, 4-9.

gia. These graduates of Princeton and Middlebury were greatly assisted by the Pennsylvanians Robert Cunningham (a graduate of Dickinson), John Newton, and Francis Cummins; and by the South Carolinians Moses Waddel and John Brown.[5]

Like the more famous Methodist circuit riders, these early members of Hopewell made constant efforts to supply all their churches and to answer every call made to them for ministerial aid throughout their wide extended bounds. Often they beat their way through unbroken forests or over wilderness trails to fill their appointments. Whenever there were sermons to be preached, prayers to be said, blessings to be asked, ordinances to be administered, or funerals to be preached, the devoted ministers of Hopewell were ever ready to perform these services. Sometimes in making their circuit, they were in danger of Indians and at least two of them lost their lives as a result of their performing their ministerial duties. In 1798 John Springer, being caught in a shower of rain at the burial of John Talbot, died a few days later of chills and fever.[6] In 1817 Dr. Robert Finley set out from Athens on a hot and dusty road and in the "sickly season, and indeed, while a bilious epidemic was considerably prevalent in some of the lower counties," and thereby "imbibed the seeds of a disease that cut short his useful labours." He returned home, sickened, and died October 3, 1817.[7]

On this last excursion this faithful old Presbyterian was gone six weeks and preached sixteen sermons. But he did more. He attended Hopewell Presbytery that met at Madison in September, 1817, and interested that body in the establishment of a theological seminary to train more ministers, for truly the laborers were few and the field of harvest seemed boundless. For carrying into effect the plans for the proposed seminary, the Presbytery appointed Drs. Finley, John Brown, and Francis Cummins as a committee to draft a report for the next session. In consequence of the death

---

5. James Stacy, *A History of the Presbyterian Church in Georgia* (Atlanta, 1912), 12-25. Hereinafter cited as Stacy, *Presbyterian Church in Georgia.*

6. *Ibid.,* 18-20. See also John S. Wilson, *The Dead of the Synod of Georgia: Necrology, or Memorials of Deceased Ministers* (Atlanta, 1869), 18. Hereinafter cited as Wilson, *Necrology.*

7. Wilson, *Necrology,* 21; Coulter, *College Life,* 41-42.

of Dr. Finley, the committee did nothing, and the theological school was never founded.[8]

In 1823 the Presbytery of Hopewell, still realizing the need of furnishing educational opportunities for training their ministers, invited the Georgia Presbytery, the only other one at that time in the state, to cooperate with them in an effort to provide the necessary theological courses. As a result, a convention was called in August, 1824. Its most important work was the organization of the Georgia Education Society, whose objective was to afford the money or other means to "pious" young men who wished to become ministers. Though the Society was chiefly under the influence and control of the Presbyterians, it was non-sectarian. Of its seven vice-presidents two were Baptists and one was a Methodist. These denominations did not cooperate to any great extent. However, the Society assisted many worthy young men in obtaining an education.[9] Alexander H. Stephens, who in his youth intended to become a minister, was aided during his four years at the University of Georgia by the Society.[10]

The Georgia Education Society found other means to help deserving students. In 1833 it organized a Manual Labor School near Athens. Dr. James Stacy, the historian of Georgia Presbyterianism, points out: "The object of this school was not only to train the mind but also to develop the body, and at the same time, lessen the expense of the students, by the products of the farm and work shop."[11] This school never proved successful and in 1834 was disbanded.

The following October the Education Society established two other manual labor schools: one at Lawrenceville called the Gwinnett Institute and the other at Midway, a village near Milledgeville, known as Midway Seminary. The Gwinnett Institute survived ten years, but the Midway Seminary proved a failure almost from the beginning and was turned over to Hopewell Presbytery

8. Wilson, *Necrology*, 21-23.
9. Stacy, *Presbyterian Church in Georgia*, 108-109.
10. Richard Malcolm Johnston and William H. Browne, *Life of Alexander H. Stephens* (Philadelphia, 1883), 51, 53.
11. *Presbyterian Church in Georgia*, 109.

after only one year's operation. Immediately the Presbytery appointed a Board of Trustees to consider converting the Seminary into a college.[12]

When the Trustees met in the Milledgeville Masonic Hall in October, 1835, they decided that they would continue the operation of the Midway Seminary and simply add a collegiate department, which would furnish the long desired facilities for training young men for the Presbyterian ministry. They recommended that the manual labor feature be continued in the Seminary and planned to try it in the college, but it was soon found to be unprofitable.[13] In February, 1837, it was discontinued in the preparatory school, and henceforth the Midway Seminary was a strictly classical institution.[14]

After settling the fate of the Seminary, the Trustees sought and obtained a charter for their proposed college. On December 21, 1835, the General Assembly of Georgia granted the charter under the title of Oglethorpe University, but it was a university only in name.[15] It had no endowment, no college buildings, no apparatus, and no faculty. Its only physical assets were a little tract of land and a few pine trees. But its Trustees were well satisfied with this humble beginning and were especially pleased with the location they had found for the University. One of them later explained that Midway was chosen with "reference to its healthfulness, and its centrality and accessibleness from all parts of the state, and of the Southern States in general. It is near the great thoroughfare from New Orleans to the North, and within a few miles of the line of the Central Rail Road, from Savannah to the West, thus bringing the seaboard and the mountains to its doors."

"The Midway Hill," he continued, "is an elevated region, traversing from West to East, abounding in botanical and mineral productions; . . . and terminating in a bold bluff on the Oconee River; at a point where are the picturesque ruins of Old Fort Wilkinson, one mile and a half from the University. The hill affords

---

12. Annual Report of the Board of Trustees of Oglethorpe University in *Minutes of the Synod of Georgia, 1847* (Milledgeville, 1848), 36.
13. T. Minutes, 1835-70, pp. 1-10.
14. *Minutes of the Synod of Georgia*, 1847, p. 36.
15. *Acts of the General Assembly of Georgia*, 1835, p. 163.

an abundant supply of pure, cold water. The foundation of the College is on a level with the summit of the cupola on the State House. The view from the cupola of the College is highly impressive, commanding a prospect for twenty miles around, in a beautifully undulating country, of the most varied and romantic kind, abounding in hill, valley and forest, with the city of Milledgeville in full view."[16]

The Trustees were anxious not only to safeguard the health of the students: they must also protect them against contaminating influences. The capital city of Milledgeville was "known for its immorality and corruption, but Midway was, after all, two miles away, and its atmosphere was considered moral and safe."[17] The charter of the University forbade "any person to establish, keep or maintain any store or shop of any description for vending any species of merchandise, groceries or confectioneries" within a mile and a half of the University.[18]

The Trustees, having selected a site that they considered both healthful and free from demoralizing influences, named a committee to send out circular letters to adjoining states, explaining the work of the University, and seeking their aid. The Reverend Messrs. Charles W. Howard and Samuel K. Talmage were appointed to solicit subscriptions. An Executive Committee of five members was elected, to whom were entrusted the planning of the new buildings and the management and control of the Manual Labor School. The Committee was also authorized to buy more land, if necessary.[19] To help raise the building fund, the Trustees decided to lay out streets at Midway and to sell lots.[20] It was further resolved that when $75,000 was subscribed, the first installment should be demanded.[21] By August, 1836, the necessary pledges had been made, and the Executive Committee was ready to begin building the long-planned University.[22]

---

16. William C. Richards, ed., *Georgia Illustrated* (Penfield, 1842), 7.
17. Aubrey Harrison Starke, *Sidney Lanier: A Biographical and Critical Study* (Chapel Hill, 1933), 21.
18. *Acts of the General Assembly of Georgia*, 1835, p. 163.
19. T. Minutes, 1835-70, pp. 5-6.
20. *Southern Recorder*, April 11, 1836.
21. T. Minutes, 1835-70, p. 6.
22. Richards, ed., *Georgia Illustrated*, 7.

When the Board of Trustees met again in November, they decided to organize the University with a president, a vice-president, three professors, and a tutor. The president and vice-president were each to be paid $2500 per annum and the professors $2000. In addition to their other duties the president, vice-president, and chaplain were to assist in instructing the students.[23]

The Board then elected a faculty:

President and Professor of Chemistry and Natural Philosophy, Carlisle Pollock Beman
Vice-President and Professor of Belles Lettres and Mental Philosophy, Eugenius Aristides Nisbet
Professor of Ancient Languages, Samuel Kennedy Talmage
Professor of Mathematics and Astronomy, Nathaniel Macon Crawford
Chaplain and Lecturer, Charles Wallace Howard

All accepted except the vice-president.[24]

At a later meeting of the Board, the Executive and Building committees were merged into one, which was afterwards known as the Prudential Committee. It was instructed to secure the services of an architect in drawing plans and specifications of the college buildings and to proceed at once to the erection of the main building, which was to be known as Central Hall. The contract was for $38,800, one tenth to be paid at the completion of each story, one tenth when the roof was put on, and the balance when the whole was completed. The first installment had been paid when the contract was let.[25]

Within a few months the construction of Central Hall had progressed far enough to lay the cornerstone. This was of solid granite, approximately 28 inches long and 22 inches wide. Cut in it was a rectangular niche for a metal box in which were deposited relics and memorials of the day. These included copies of the *Southern Recorder*, March 28, 1837; the *Georgia Journal*, March 28, 1837; the *Federal Union*, March 28, 1837; the *Standard*

---

23. T. Minutes, 1835-70, p. 8.
24. *Ibid.*, 10-15. Apparently the office was abandoned as it was not mentioned again in the Minutes.
25. *Ibid.*, 31, 32, 35-36.

of Union, March 21, 1837; a drawing on sheepskin of General Oglethorpe; a silver quarter; and a silver half dime.[26]

On Saturday, March 31, 1837, the Presbytery of Hopewell, being in session at Milledgeville, assembled at Midway for the laying of the cornerstone. Judge Joseph H. Lumpkin was invited to deliver the principal address, and the Masons were asked to participate in the exercises. The procession started at Steward Hall and proceeded to the northeast corner of the foundation of the new building, where it halted. After a prayer by one of the Presbytery, the Masons placed the cornerstone in position "in due and ample form." Before the exercises were over, a hard rain came and prevented the address of Judge Lumpkin. Later in the day he delivered it at the Methodist Church in Milledgeville.[27]

By the end of the year enough buildings had been finished to begin instruction.[28] At that time twelve dormitories had been erected. These were one story wooden structures, with two rooms each, eighteen by eighteen feet, arranged in rows twelve feet apart on either side of the campus. The other buildings included the President's house, the Academy, and a wooden chapel, which could be used for a recitation room.[29]

When on January 1, 1838, Oglethorpe opened its doors, one hundred and twenty-five students enrolled in the College and the Seminary together.[30] The report of the Prudential Committee showed that the school was off to a good start: The total subscriptions to date were $72,190, of which $18,512 had been paid;

26. In 1921 some workmen who were excavating at the site of the University found the stone buried deep in the earth. When the metal box was opened, the above named relics were found. Leola Selman Beeson, *Sidney Lanier at Oglethorpe* (Macon, 1936), 39. See Minutes of Benevolent Lodge, No. 6, 1837-1864, p. 12. In the Milledgeville Masonic Hall.

27. Joseph Henry Lumpkin, *An Address delivered before Hopewell Presbytery, the Board of Trustees of Oglethorpe University . . .* (Milledgeville, 1837), 1.

28. *Southern Recorder*, Dec. 10, 1837; Stacy, *Presbyterian Church in Georgia*, 111; Richards, ed., *Georgia Illustrated*, 8.

29. George White, *Statistics of the State of Georgia* (Savannah, 1849), 78; *idem, Historical Collections of Georgia* (New York, 1854), 266; Richards, ed., *Georgia Illustrated*, 8.

30. T. Minutes, 1835-70, p. 35. Unfortunately the Minutes do not record how many were enrolled in each department. Probably there were few more than 25 in the college, as in 1841 there were only 31. *American Almanac,* 1841, p. 151. See also Stacy, *Presbyterian Church in Georgia*, 113.

the University owned 500 acres of land; and Midway was fast becoming a college town, as is shown by the sale of lots amounting to several thousand dollars.[31] Commenting on Oglethorpe's auspicious beginning, an alumnus of the University later wrote, "The Esprit de corps was excellent, the health of the students fine, the discipline firm. The zeal, fidelity and ability of the faculty were highly complimented . . . . In fine, it was a matter of general congratulation that the outlook was so bright and encouraging."[32]

From the first the influence of the University was elevating and beneficial to both Midway and Milledgeville. Before Oglethorpe had been in operation five months, people from the two communities began attending programs sponsored by the school. At the end of the first year there was no commencement as there were no graduates, but President Beman invited "the friends, patrons, and public at large" to attend the closing exercises. Its main features were the junior and sophomore oratorical contests.[33]

The second year began under as favorable prospects as the first. Professor Howard returned from Europe with $1,500 worth of scientific equipment purchased from subscriptions that he had raised in the North. The Prudential Committee was so optimistic that it proposed to endow a new chair in the University to be known as the Beman professorship. The money for it was to be raised by the payment of $500 each by fifty patrons of the school. In fact, several had already expressed their willingness to do this.[34] The college enrollment was slightly increased and the school could now boast of its first senior class, of four members. They were graduated November 10, 1839.[35]

In the meantime work on Central Hall continued. In August, 1840, it was completed. Shortly thereafter one of the Oglethorpe professors thus described the new building: "It is a brick structure, painted white, two stories high, besides a basement. It is constructed after the Grecian-Doric order, without and within. The central part contains the finest College chapel in the United States;

---

31. T. Minutes, 1835-70, p. 38.
32. Stacy, *Presbyterian Church in Georgia*, 113.
33. *Southern Recorder*, April 17, 1838; Oct. 9, 1838.
34. T. Minutes, 1835-70, pp. 37-38.
35. *Ibid.*, 49; *Southern Recorder*, Nov. 5, 1839.

its whole dimensions are 52 feet front by 89 feet deep, including a colonnade 14 feet deep, supported by four massive pillars, and the vestibule to the chapel is 11 feet deep. The dimensions of the chapel are 48 feet by 60 in the main story, and 48 by 71 in the gallery, the latter extending over the vestibule. The ceiling of the chapel is in the form of an elliptical arch, resting on a rich cornice, and containing a chaste and original centre piece. Attached to the building are two wings, 30 feet front by 34 deep, and three stories high; making the entire front of the edifice 112 feet in length. Each story in the wings is divided into a professor's office in front, and a recitation or lecture room in the rear. There are in the basement story and wings sixteen rooms, affording ample accommodations for library, museum, apparatus and all other conveniences for College purposes."[36]

Hardly had Central Hall been completed when President Beman resigned in November, 1840. He was dissatisfied because the Trustees would not allow him to flog students above the sophomore year. Furthermore he favored the New School theology that just then was beginning to divide the whole Presbyterian church, North and South. Beman had come to Midway in 1834 as rector of the Manual Labor School when it was first established by Hopewell Presbytery. Largely under his leadership Oglethorpe was born and grew to a position of permanence and importance throughout the state.[37] Before coming to Midway, he had already taught some of Georgia's leading sons: Hugh A. Haralson,[38] Henry L. Benning,[39] and John G. Shorter.[40] Upon them and many others who came under his tutelage at Oglethorpe he had left the stamp of his own stern character. A young co-teacher with him who was destined to become Governor of Georgia later wrote:

In his day Dr. Beman was regarded as the Nestor of education throughout the South. He had unusual gifts as a teacher and a disci-

---

36. Dr. Talmage in Richards, ed., *Georgia Illustrated*, 7-8.
37. William J. Northen, ed., *Men of Mark in Georgia* (7 vols. Atlanta, 1906-1912), II, 96. See also T. Minutes, 1835-70, p. 67; Stacy, *Presbyterian Church in Georgia*, 115, 183-186.
38. Northen, ed., *Men of Mark in Georgia*, II, 34.
39. *Ibid.*, III, 260.
40. *History of the Baptist Denomination in Georgia, with Biographical Compendium* (Atlanta, 1881), Part II, p. 479. Shorter was born in Georgia, but after moving to Alabama became its governor.

plinarian. He had thorough knowledge of human nature, and almost unerring judgment of character. His methods of instruction were most thorough and his government and school discipline were firm and positive. He would not for a moment tolerate or excuse disobedience to authority or the questioning of his right to govern. He never exacted more than was just and due, but he was sure to obtain all he called for in conduct and study. When these results were not reached for the asking, they were always secured through compulsion.

Dr. Beman made no distinction among his pupils as to discipline. The young and the old; the elementary and the advanced were all brought under the rod if they could not be controlled without it. He was a man of great physical courage and determined purpose. No bad conduct ever escaped his notice, nor did the perpetration of evil deeds ever escape punishment. His methods put into practice for this day would be considered severe, but it cannot be denied that he made many good citizens of very bad boys who were beyond control in their homes and such as had become disturbing elements in the communities from which they came.

So wrote Governor William J. Northen of the first president of Oglethorpe University.[41]

41. Northen, ed., *Men of Mark in Georgia*, II, 97.

CHAPTER II

The Struggle to Survive

PRESIDENT Beman, upon his resignation from Oglethorpe, removed to La Grange and there established an academy, continuing the kind of work that he was best suited to do by experience and training.[1] He was never temperamentally qualified to be the head of a college, and he left behind few students to regret his departure. His stern discipline and austere manner were better requisites for governing and teaching youngsters in a preparatory school than the religious youth who attended Oglethorpe. One of the University students thought him "less man than devil," and another never forgot his terrifying countenance. Maturer years usually changed the young men's estimate of "Old Beman," as they privately called him. When he was traveling in the West in 1858, he visited Robert W. Jemison, a member of the class that was graduated in 1840 when President Beman resigned. Jemison, now editor of the Monroe (Louisiana) *Register*, looking back on his college days and the first president of Oglethorpe, said of him: "Many men there be, who have made more noise in the world than he, but few, very few, whose influence has been more felt, and that for good."[2]

All along the Trustees had appreciated the head of the University and accepted his resignation with reluctance. To fill his place was no easy task, as they were soon to learn. At first they elected the Reverend John Breckinridge, a noted Presbyterian minister and theologian, but he declined, leaving the institution without a president for a whole year. Until the position could be permanently filled, Professor Samuel K. Talmage was made chairman of the faculty.[3] Under his leadership the University resumed

---

1. Northen, ed., *Men of Mark in Georgia*, II, 96.
2. *Federal Union*, May 4, 1858; see also *ibid.*, June 1, 1858.
3. T. Minutes, 1835-70, pp. 67, 69.

operation in January, 1841, and continued to merit the reputation and respect it had maintained when Beman guided it. At the end of the school year the *Southern Recorder*, a Milledgeville weekly, applauded the progress that Oglethorpe was making under its temporary head: "This young Institution is silently, quietly, and surely advancing in its march of usefulness and in public confidence."[4]

While Professor Talmage was proving his administrative ability, the Trustees continued to look for someone to take the place of Beman. After Breckinridge declined the offer, they tried to effect a merger of Oglethorpe with the Theological Seminary at Columbia, South Carolina, with the understanding that the latter school should move to Midway and, of course, bring its president, who would head the combined institutions. When this proposal failed, the Board offered the synods of South Carolina, Alabama, Mississippi, and Florida the privilege of nominating the incumbent if they would endow professorships at Oglethorpe, but it was stipulated that they might withdraw their support if the University should ever pass from Presbyterian control. When the synods of the neighboring states refused the Board's offer, a committee was appointed to confer with Dr. Alonzo Church, president of the University of Georgia, and to invite him to accept the presidency of Oglethorpe. Dr. Church was too well satisfied to make a change, and the Trustees had to look elsewhere to fill the vacancy. By that time Professor Talmage had completed a successful college year and had demonstrated his executive talents so well that it suddenly occurred to the Trustees that there in their midst was the man for whom they had been searching all the time. In November, 1841, at a meeting of the Synod of Georgia and South Carolina at Charleston, they named Samuel Kennedy Talmage the second president of Oglethorpe University.[5]

The Trustees could not have realized then how happy a choice they had made. Talmage was destined to guide the college for the next twenty-four years through financial adversity, a long period of prosperity, and finally war. Only death would rob the school

4. Nov. 16, 1841.
5. T. Minutes, 1835-70, pp. 66-75.

of his excellent qualities of leadership. In 1841, at the time of his appointment, he was at the height of his physical and mental powers. He was a man of small stature, with curly brown hair and sparkling blue eyes. Like ministers of his day, he usually wore a dark black broadcloth suit and carried a gold-headed cane.[6]

A few days before Dr. Talmage was made president, one observer characterized him as "a learned and eloquent divine, graceful in his deportment, and of persevering energetic habits. The ability and devotion with which he has given himself to the rearing of this infant institution is worthy of all commendation. Self-sacrificing and conscientious, and dedicated as he is to the cause of religion and literature; a discerning public will not fail to appreciate and reward his labor of love."[7] He never lost the confidence and respect of the students, faculty, Trustees, or the public at large, and his influence was felt far beyond the college campus. In 1845 Princeton conferred a Doctor of Divinity degree on him in recognition of his outstanding work as an educational leader.[8] When he was nearing the end of his career, he was as beloved as when he assumed the duties of his office. Typical of the public praise that he regularly received is this eulogy written in 1860: "The Rev. Dr. Talmage, the President, is popular with the students, as he is with all who know him personally. Thorough in learning and skilful in discipline, he is the model of a finished character - 'the scholar, the gentleman, and the christian.' "[9]

Professor Talmage was a native of New Jersey and a graduate of Princeton. He was born near Somerville on December 11, 1798, the sixth son of Thomas Talmage, Sr., and Mary McCoy. In infancy he was baptized in the Presbyterian faith and grew up "in the nurture and admonition of the Lord." To earn money to attend college, he began teaching at the age of seventeen. At twenty he entered Princeton and was graduated in 1820. After

6. Sarah Cantey Whitaker Allen, "Old Oglethorpe University—Midway, Georgia," 50. An unpublished typescript in the possession of Miss Floride Allen, of Midway.
7. *Southern Recorder*, Nov. 16, 1841.
8. *Ibid.*, July 8, 1845.
9. *Ibid.*, July 27, 1860.

SAMUEL KENNEDY TALMAGE

From a photograph

NATHANIEL MACON CRAWFORD
From a steel engraving

two years of teaching in private schools, he returned to his Alma Mater to be a tutor and at the same time to study in the Theological Seminary. He finished his course in 1825 and was ordained by the Presbytery of Newton as an evangelist. Coming South, he was a missionary for a year at Hamburg and other points in Edgefield District, South Carolina. In 1827 he began to assist the Reverend S. S. Davis with the duties of his pastorate in the First Presbyterian Church in Augusta, Georgia, just across the Savannah from Hamburg. When the Reverend Mr. Davis retired, young Talmage was called to the full-time ministry of the church, and continued from 1828 until 1836 when he and Dr. C. W. Howard became financial agents of Oglethorpe.[10]

While he was pastor in Augusta, he was once called to the bedside of a member of his church, Miss Ruth Sterritt, who was seriously ill. Her nurse was a widow to whom she had promised to give all of her jewels, and to whose son her pony, if she should die. When the pastor came, Miss Sterritt offered him a glass of the wine that her doctor had prescribed. Not being circumscribed by present-day conventions that forbid a minister's drinking wine, the young preacher poured out a glass full and drank it. On his way home he suddenly became "ill" or more probably slightly intoxicated. Blaming the wine for his condition, he sent a messenger to the mother of the sick woman and urged her not to give any more of it to her daughter. The wine was analyzed and said to contain prussic acid. The nurse was accused of trying to poison Miss Sterritt and was threatened with arrest, but she escaped and was never heard of again. Miss Sterritt slowly recovered and was an invalid for many months. Henceforth she lived in constant dread that someone was trying to poison her, and she trusted few people.[11]

Because she thought her pastor had saved her life, she fell in love with him, and the couple were married on July 11, 1834.[12] After they moved to Midway, Mrs. Talmage became increasingly a recluse and apparently suffered from paranoia. Only a few close

10. T. Minutes, 1835-70, p. 238; Wilson, *Necrology*, 283-286.
11. Allen, "Old Oglethorpe University," 52.
12. Wilson, *Necrology*, 290.

friends were welcomed into her home. She never bore any children to keep her company, but she found pleasure and companionship in her cats of which she had a great number, but never any to spare. When one of them was missing, she even called on the Oglethorpe students to help her find it. One young man received the following note from her:

Mr. Thomas Whitaker—
    If a kitten almost grown has strayed into the campus rooms you will greatly oblige me by reclaiming it for me. It is yellow and white and is an especial pet of mine.
R. W. TALMAGE

I thought I heard it cry out in the direction of one of the dormitories today.[13]

While Mrs. Talmage worried over her cats, her husband considered far weightier matters. As the new president of Oglethorpe University, he found his duties and responsibilities many and varied. He inherited from Professor Beman the problem of developing in the college students the feeling that they were young gentlemen and should act as such. Unlike Beman, he did not believe in maintaining discipline by flogging and other extreme methods of punishment that were commonly practiced in that day both by colleges and secondary schools. He secured discipline and respect by employing methods that are quite modern even today. He understood the psychology of youth and applied it in dealing with the Oglethorpe boys. He realized that they were not adult and should not be expected to behave like grown people. And he had a sense of humor that every teacher needs.

One night several of the boys planned to play a practical joke on him by pulling his carriage two miles from the college to the top of Smith's Mount and leaving it there. Dr. Talmage, hearing of their design, decided to enter into the prank by concealing himself in the carriage before they arrived. He kept still and quiet until they reached their destination. Just as they were ready to leave, he rose up and called out, "Now, boys, I have enjoyed the

---

13. Allen, "Old Oglethorpe University," 52.

ride here; please take me home." The students were surprised and chagrined. Seeing the joke was now turned on them, they good-naturedly took the college president back to his front gate, where he alighted. Politely bowing, he thanked them for his enjoyable ride home. Then the students put the carriage in the barn and resolved never again to try that kind of fun.[14]

Dr. Talmage was profoundly religious and conceived of his chief duty in life as preaching the Gospel and urging people to turn from their sins to God. He could not think of education divorced from the Christian religion. His religious work during his twenty-five years as head of the University was as evident as his educational leadership. He not only conducted daily chapel exercises at the college, but also traveled over Georgia and even into other states to preach Christ, to perform marriage ceremonies, or to bury the dead. He was the most popular minister in Baldwin County and was often called to Milledgeville to participate in such public functions as the Fourth of July celebrations, or a joint session of the General Assembly at the state capitol.[15] After the Georgia Insane Asylum was established just two miles from the college, he sometimes preached to the inmates who were sufficiently rational to understand his message.

One afternoon he preached to them on God's pardon of the sinner. To illustrate how He sent Jesus into the world to save the lost, Dr. Talmage told a story of a murderer who had been sentenced to be hanged. Some of the friends of the condemned man, he related, appealed to the Governor for a pardon, but an answer was delayed in coming. Dr. Talmage then went into minute detail to describe how on the day of execution the sheriff took the accused from the jail, seated him on his coffin, and drove him to the gallows. Descending the scaffold, the sheriff raised his hand to spring the trigger, which would send the condemned man to his death. Suddenly the sheriff heard the sound of galloping hoofs in the distance, and, turning his head, he saw a horseman coming at full speed and holding something high in his hand. When he

---

14. *Ibid.*, 50.
15. *Southern Recorder*, 1840-1865, *passim.*

came nearer, he cried, "Pardon! pardon! do not hang that man. I have a pardon for him!"

At that point in the story Dr. Talmage digressed to picture the rider furiously spurring his horse and leaning forward in the saddle, anxiously hurrying to get the Governor's orders to the sheriff. Then the preacher described the horse stretching every nerve and tendon, with nostrils distended and sides heaving. To one of the mental patients in the audience the graphically-pictured scene became a living reality and at length in his impatience at the minister's tardiness to come to the point, he sprang up and exclaimed, "O! Dr. Talmage, do be in a hurry or that poor man will be hung before you get his pardon to him." The whole congregation was thrown into such an uproar that the service was terminated abruptly without singing or the benediction. When the college boys heard of the incident they were greatly amused.[16]

Dr. Talmage was well qualified to direct the educational program of the University and to guide the students in spiritual matters, but he found that managing the finances of the institution, so as to keep it from closing its doors, required all his skill as well as that of the Trustees and friends of Oglethorpe. Before he became president, indebtedness had already begun to be a great embarrassment to the University authorities, and was another reason for Beman's resignation. In the summer of 1838, when the construction of Central Hall began, only $18,516 out of $72,190 subscriptions had been paid. As the work progressed, the pecuniary difficulties increased, and in November, 1839, the Trustees noted: "A crisis has arrived in which the fate of the institution turns on the conduct of its friends . . . . Great enterprises are not accomplished without great efforts and ours must correspond with the greatness of the object and the embarrassment of the times."[17]

At this meeting the Board, hoping to divide its responsibility and also to secure a larger number of supporters, recommended that the Presbytery of Hopewell, which was sponsoring the college, tender a transfer of control of Oglethorpe to the Synod of

---

16. Stacy, *Presbyterian Church in Georgia*, 321-322.
17. T. Minutes, 1835-70, pp. 55-56.

Georgia and South Carolina.[18] In November, 1839, the Presbytery unanimously granted the request and the Synod unanimously accepted the supervision of the University. Thus supported by the patronage of the Synod and assisted financially by the efforts of an enlarged number of agents, Oglethorpe began the year 1840 under seemingly bright prospects. Thinking their difficulties past, the Trustees congratulated themselves and the friends of the University on their great success in relieving it of its pecuniary embarrassment. They were especially pleased with the Reverend Remembrance Chamberlain, the Fiscal Agent of the college, whose efforts had been rewarded "in the most satisfactory manner."[19]

The Trustees rejoiced too soon. As noted earlier, Central Hall was completed in August, 1840. One tenth of the contract for $38,800 had been paid at the completion of each story; another tenth when the roof was put on; and now that the building was finished, the balance was due to the contractor, Joseph Lane, but the Board was unable to meet this obligation. Before the end of the year funds were not available even to meet current expenses, and the Prudential Committee found it necessary to borrow money to pay the salaries of the faculty. So matters stood when Beman resigned and Talmage was made chairman of the faculty.[20]

The new president immediately after his election met with the Board of Trustees in a meeting called for the purpose of discussing the financial condition of the University. At this time it appeared that several friends of the school had advanced large sums that saved it from bankruptcy. Those who contributed most were Joseph Lane, Miller Grieve, and Richard J. Nichols. Without their assistance the University would have failed before it had been in operation three years.[21]

Joseph Lane was a native of Portland, Maine, and should hardly have been expected to be interested in building up a college in Georgia, but from his New England background he inherited

---

18. *Ibid.*, 57-58.
19. *Ibid.*, 62.
20. *Ibid.*, 66-70, 77.
21. *Ibid.*, 77.

a respect for higher education that made him one of Oglethorpe's best friends. In 1834 he moved to Midway to build a fine home for Colonel Samuel Rockwell (later the mansion occupied by Governor Herschel V. Johnson). This house, which is still standing and is generally considered the most beautiful in Baldwin County, won for him an enviable reputation as both an architect and a builder. In 1838, when the contract for Central Hall was to be let, the Trustees naturally turned to him. He did an excellent job in the construction of this building, which became widely admired as an architectural masterpiece.[22] He received little more than half of the price agreed upon in the contract, but that did not turn him against the University. He patiently waited for the small amounts that he did receive, and when he died in 1842, he was still due nearly $20,000, a large sum for that day. When the Thalian Literary Society built a new hall in 1859-1860, his son, Joseph Lane, Jr., took the contract though he too failed to collect in full.[23]

Equally, if not more, generous than Joseph Lane were Miller Grieve and Richard J. Nichols, each of whom gave from first to last an estimated sum of $30,000. These two philanthropists were staunch Presbyterians, who hoped to see Oglethorpe become in the South what Princeton was in the North. Grieve was a native of Edinburgh, Scotland, who emigrated to Lexington, Georgia, in his youth. In 1829, when he was twenty-seven years old, he moved to Milledgeville to be secretary to Governor George R. Gilmer.[24] Here in the state capital he met and married Sarah Grantland. From his wife's paternal uncle he bought the *Southern Recorder*, Georgia's leading newsweekly.[25] In this paper he advertised Oglethorpe from its founding until its removal to Atlanta. During a period when local news was minimized, he recorded the important (and many unimportant) happenings at the

---

22. Cf. Richards, ed., *Georgia Illustrated*, 7.
23. Allen, "Old Oglethorpe University," 15, 21; Thalian Minutes, *passim.* Date of Joseph Lane's death copied from his tombstone in the Milledgeville Cemetery.
24. Allen, "Old Oglethorpe University," 20.
25. Anna Maria Green Cook, *History of Baldwin County, Georgia* (Anderson, S. C., 1925), 347.

MANSION OF HERSCHEL V. JOHNSON

Built by Joseph Lane, circa 1834

THE HOME OF DR. TALMAGE AT MIDWAY

From a photograph in the possession of Miss Floride Allen

University so that a file of this weekly from 1835-1870 is the best source of historical information on the school. The value of this free advertising was incalculable.

In addition to their contributions Nichols and Grieve advanced large sums of money as a loan to the University. To secure these amounts, the Trustees executed a mortgage on "all the property real and personal" belonging to Oglethorpe. This was done in April, 1842, and for the next four years the college authorities were little worried by financial matters.[26] As an alumnus later explained, "Under the quieting influence of the mortgage, and through the activity of a number of agents, and with the contributions of churches, and gifts of friends as well as patience of creditors, the Institution was kept afloat."[27] The day of reckoning was merely put off, for the indebtedness of the University continued to increase gradually each year until a crisis was reached in the fall of 1846. By that time the debt included the mortgage held by Nichols and Grieve, the unpaid balance to the heirs of Joseph Lane, a note of $6,507.38 due the Central Bank, the delinquent monthly salaries of the professors, and several other claims, totaling nearly $70,000. At the annual meeting of the Board of Trustees, Grieve discussed a plan of liquidating all of Oglethorpe's obligations by compromise. The Trustees readily concurred and agreed to offer the creditors twenty-five per cent on each claim. All except one—the Georgia State Penitentiary— settled by accepting ten to sixty-five per cent, the average being twenty-five. Thus $69,739.01 was compromised in 1849 for $17,-633.91.[28]

---

26. T. Minutes, 1835-70, p. 77.
27. Stacy, *Presbyterian Church in Georgia*, 118.
28. See T. Minutes, 1835-70, p. 127. The compromises effected were as follows:

Creditor	Claim	Compromise
Joseph Lane	$17,464.85	$ 5,000.00
Abner Cragin	3,714.98	928.75
R. J. Nichols	20,724.49	5,181.12
M. Grieve	14,966.83	4,176.55
B. T. Bethune	4,170.13	600.00
Central Bank	6,507.38	650.74
Georgia Penitentiary	713.60	————
N. M. Crawford	1,576.75	1,096.75
Totals	**$69,739.01**	**$17,633.91**

The unfortunate financial struggle, which had lasted for ten years, had a disastrous effect upon maintaining a faculty. During this period there were many resignations and the Trustees found it difficult to get qualified professors when there were such poor prospects of paying their salaries. In 1839 Nathaniel Macon Crawford, professor of mathematics and astronomy, resigned because the Trustees could not pay his salary in full. Ten years later when the great financial compromise was made, the Board still owed him $1,576.75. He settled for $1,096.75, but had to wait for his money.[29]

In the resignation of Professor Crawford, Oglethorpe lost one of the ablest men ever connected with the institution in its entire history. He was the son of the famous William H. Crawford, who was successively United States senator, secretary of war, and Presidential candidate in 1824. His mother was the daughter of Louis Gerdine, a French immigrant, who settled at Beech Island, South Carolina. Until Macon (he was called by his middle name) was fourteen, he spent much time in Washington, D. C. At fifteen he entered the sophomore class of Franklin College, better known now as the University of Georgia. Leading his class for three years, he was graduated with first honor in 1829 in the famous class with Robert Toombs, Bishop George Pierce, Bishop Thomas F. Scott, Dr. Shaler Hillyer, and Dr. John N. Waddel, chancellor of the University of Mississippi. After leaving college, he studied law in his father's office and was admitted to the bar, but never practiced the legal profession. During Governor George R. Gilmer's administration he moved to Milledgeville to serve as clerk of the executive department. While in this office, in 1837, he was elected professor of mathematics in Oglethorpe University. Though he was only twenty-six years old when he began teaching, he was easily the equal of any member of the faculty in mental acumen and an unbounded thirst for knowledge. Dr. Talmage spoke of him as "a walking literary cyclopedia," and often consulted him for information.[30]

---

29. *Ibid.*, 51, 127.
30. Northen, ed., *Men of Mark in Georgia*, II, 334.

Professor Crawford was reared in the Presbyterian church and in early life became a member of that denomination. While he was teaching at Oglethorpe, the birth of his first child led him to examine the subject of infant baptism. He became convinced that that practice was not scriptural, and inquiring further, he came to believe that immersion was the only mode of that ordinance taught in the New Testament. Disrupting the ties that bound him to his Presbyterian brethren, he joined the Baptist church and in 1844 was ordained to the ministry of that religious body. After serving as pastor of two churches, he accepted the chair of Biblical Literature in Mercer University, and in 1854 became its president. Resigning this position, he taught for two years in the University of Mississippi, but came back to Georgia before the War Between the States. Again he was president of Mercer, 1858-1865. At the close of the war, he went to Kentucky to be the president of Georgetown College and held this position until failing health caused him to resign in 1871. Besides his educational work, he was editor of *The Christian Index*, a frequent contributor to the religious press, and author of *Christian Paradoxes* (Nashville, 1858).[31]

In May, 1839, six months before Professor Crawford withdrew from Oglethorpe, Professor Charles W. Howard sent his resignation to the Trustees, stating that he had learned from "responsible sources" that his holding a professorship in the University was "creating in the minds of many persons a prejudice against this Institution."[32] His letter referred to the controversy over the Rescinding Act of 1837, which he was actively opposing. The dissension grew out of a plan of union between the Presbyterians and Congregationalists, formed in 1800, but after thirty-seven years rescinded and declared unconstitutional by the Presbyterian General Assembly. Dr. Howard and many others throughout Georgia and the nation considered the action of the Assembly

---

31. *Ibid.*, 333. *History of the Baptist Denomination in Georgia with Biographical Compendium and Portrait Gallery of Baptist Ministers and Other Georgia Baptists* (Atlanta, 1881), Part II, pp. 154-157. Edwin A. Alderman and Joel Chandler Harris, eds., *Library of Southern Literature* (17 vols., Atlanta, 1906-1923), XV, 100.
32. T. Minutes, 1835-70, p. 46.

equally unconstitutional, and showed their displeasure in 1839 when he and several other ministers withdrew from the Presbytery of Hopewell and formed an independent Presbytery, which they called Etowah.[33] At first the Trustees would not accept the resignation, but agreed to let him retire in November, 1839, at the time when Professor Crawford resigned.[34]

The University was thus deprived of two of its most talented young men after it had been in operation just two years. Born in the same year as Crawford, Howard was educated for the ministry at Princeton and ordained as pastor of the Milledgeville Presbyterian Church in 1834. The next year he became a leading spirit in establishing Oglethorpe University. He was one of its original Trustees, suggested the name of Oglethorpe for the college, and then became the most successful agent the school ever had. In one year he is said to have got subscriptions to the amount of $120,000. As chairman of a committee to raise funds, he wrote and published in 1835, *An Appeal in Behalf of Oglethorpe University*, in which he set forth the purposes of the founders of the institution. In concluding his pamphlet, he said in part:

> We appeal to the Christian. Cousin, the French philosopher, by no means blindly partial to christianity, affirms in his unequalled report, that learning must be indissolubly united with religion, or the former cannot flourish . . . .
> We feel, and it is a rock beneath our feet, that the hand of God is in this matter. He is with us, and whom shall we fear—of what shall we be afraid. We seek to advance no private interests; we labor for no pecuniary emolument; our end is the cultivation of mind, that most glorious structure of the heavenly Architect— mind, created to use its lofty powers in the study of *His* character, and in the praise of his mercies, unfatigued throughout eternity. Our end is the cultivation of the heart—the heart unregenerate, the temple of the living God. What objects more desirable? What ends more worthy of attainment? Laboring for such purposes, we look with humble confidence, to Him, the source of unerring wisdom for guidance in our work, and to His smiles,

---

33. Stacy, *Presbyterian Church in Georgia*, 183-186.
34. T. Minutes, 1835-70, p. 53.

for support when difficulty and disappointment might otherwise fright us from our duty.[35]

Professor Howard's *Appeal* was immediately heeded and within a year enough money had been raised, largely by his efforts, for the executive committee to begin planning to build the college buildings.[36] While no one man can be called the founder of Oglethorpe University, Charles W. Howard did more than any other person to deserve the honor.

There were other professors who contributed probably less than Howard, but each of whom served the University well for a few short years. John H. Fitten, the first honor graduate of the first graduating class, was elected tutor in mathematics as soon as he received his degree. He filled the place of his former teacher, Macon Crawford, with such credit that the Trustees made him a professor after just two years of tutoring (1840 through 1841). He continued until 1845, but resigned when lack of finances made it hard for the University to pay salaries.[37]

Two sons of Liberty County, Georgia, John B. Mallard and John W. Baker, taught all too few years at Oglethorpe. Mallard had been educated for the ministry, but had come to Midway to be principal of the Female Seminary. In 1841 he was elected tutor of natural philosophy at Oglethorpe, and the next year he was made a professor in the University. He was a man of fine literary taste and ability and a historian of great promise. In 1840 he published *A Short Account of the Congregational Church at Midway* [near Savannah, not the Midway in Baldwin County]. This work shows that its author not only did careful research, but also had rare charm and beauty of expression. He planned to expand this study, but unfortunately his enlarged manuscript was lost when his home was burned. This young author resigned from Oglethorpe in 1843.[38]

A year after Mallard left the University, his fellow citizen of

---

35. *An Appeal in Behalf of Oglethorpe University* (Augusta, 1835), 22-23.
36. Richards, ed., *Georgia Illustrated*, 7.
37. T. Minutes, 1835-70, pp. 75, 99.
38. James Stacy, *History of Midway Congregational Church* (Newnan, Ga., 1899), 107; T. Minutes, 1835-70, pp. 74, 95.

Liberty County, John Wycliffe Baker, was elected professor of ancient languages at Oglethorpe. Like Mallard, he traced his ancestry to Puritan New England and had grown up in a community noted for its religious zeal and intellectual achievements. He was a graduate of the University of Georgia (1832) and of Princeton Theological Seminary (1835). He came to Milledgeville after the Reverend Charles W. Howard resigned the pastorate of the Presbyterian Church, and filled his place for many years. While serving the Milledgeville church, he was elected to teach at Oglethorpe. He was a thorough classical scholar, who trained his students to appreciate Latin and Greek literature. After seven years, he resigned in 1851, greatly beloved by faculty and students. He continued his ministerial duties at Milledgeville, Marietta, Smyrna, LaFayette, and elsewhere in Georgia for over sixty years. At the time of his death he was oldest, in years of service, of all the Presbyterian ministers in the state.[39]

If Oglethorpe found difficulty in holding its faculty in the 1840's, it was fortunate in this decade in adding two professors who would teach until the University closed its doors forever at Midway. They were Charles Whitmarsh Lane and Robert Calendar Smith. Lane was the son of Joseph Lane, the architect and builder of Central Hall. When Charles was thirteen, he came with his parents to Milledgeville, where the boy grew up. He entered Oglethorpe soon after it began operation and was graduated with an A.B. degree in 1842. He was then made tutor in mathematics, and when Professor Fitten resigned in 1844, he was elected to take his place. He held this position for the next twenty-five years and was connected with Oglethorpe, as student, tutor, and professor thirty years—the longest record set by anyone. Only Dr. Talmage was a faculty member as long, but his total connection was a little shorter than Professor Lane's.

Lane especially admired the president of the college, and for a quarter of a century their association was very intimate and affectionate. Despite the disparity in their ages, the two men often were seen together. When his only son was born, Lane named

---

39. Stacy, *History of Midway Congregational Church*, 114-115.

him Samuel Talmage.[40] Partly under the influence of the president, Professor Lane was ordained to the Presbyterian ministry
in 1857. Continuing to teach, he did mission work in the area
surrounding the college, especially among the poor and lowly. It
was said of his entering the ministry: "There began its course
the zeal for Christ and for humanity which knew no let nor stay,
but flowed onward with his life's current until the ocean of
eternity received it out of man's sight."[41]

A kindred spirit with this saintly professor was the Reverend
Dr. Smith, who joined the Oglethorpe faculty in 1847 and continued until 1870 when both he and Lane resigned. Born June 7,
1810, in Cumberland County, North Carolina, Professor Smith
lived in that state for his first fifteen years. In 1825 his family
moved to Autauga County, Alabama, where under the influence
of his godly mother he determined to be a Presbyterian minister. Working to earn money to go to college, he soon had enough
to enter Miami University in Ohio and was graduated in 1837.
For the next ten years he was engaged in preaching and teaching. In 1847 he was chosen professor of moral and mental science
at Oglethorpe. As a teacher, he expounded his subject with clarity
and force and was markedly successful in arousing his students to
high scholarship and diligent work.[42] One of them wrote of him
in long retrospect: "Professor Smith was . . . a man of philosophic
mind and of great strength of character. He was very kind, though
somewhat reserved, and got nearer to the students than any of his
colleagues."[43] Like Professors Lane and Talmage, he was as anxious
to preach the gospel as to impart knowledge and frequently filled
the pulpit in churches near the college.[44]

With the addition of Professor Smith the faculty witnessed few
changes until the War Between the States. In the decade, 1852-
1861, only one professor resigned. This stability was in part, if not

---

40. Allen, "Old Oglethorpe University," 56.
41. *Ibid.*
42. *Ibid.*
43. E. M. Green in Thornwell Jacobs, *The Oglethorpe Story* (Atlanta, 1916),
    97.
44. Allen, "Old Oglethorpe University," 60.

largely, due to the fact that the University was put on a sound financial footing. After the compromise of the indebtedness in 1849, the Trustees adopted the "scholarship plan" for raising money. The scheme entitled any parent who would pay the University $100.00 the privilege of educating all his sons free. Upon the payment of $500.00 by either an individual or a group the donor would receive "a perpetual scrip," which allowed him to designate anyone whom he chose to be educated without cost of tuition. Each contributor was issued a certificate which might be inherited as any other property, and the benefits of which the heirs might claim.

As soon as the plan was adopted, the Trustees sent agents into the Southeastern states to explain it to the Presbyterians who had sons to educate. The scheme was simple and appealed to the Scotch blood in that denomination so much that by November, 1851, $60,000 had been subscribed and the Trustees ordered the issuing and signing of the certificates.[45]

This sum relieved the University of its financial embarrassment, and there followed the most prosperous decade—1852-1861—in its history. In the annual report of the Board of Trustees to the Synod of Georgia, in 1851, particular notice was made of the improved condition and the hopeful outlook for the future of Oglethorpe:

> Three years ago a debt of more than $70,000 rested upon it with overwhelming power; not a single Professorship was adequately endowed. The number of students was small; darkness, doubt and fear surrounded the institution. But such is not the present history of its condition. With the means furnished by the recent effort to raise $60,000 the entire indebtedness of the Institution for buildings, lands, and including a considerable portion of the amount due the Faculty, has been extinguished, and the entire property originally costing nearly $70,000, is relieved of all encumbrance. By the aid of this effort, the endowment of the Alabama Professorship has been completed; that of South Carolina founded; the means now remain for the endowment of a third Professorship connected with this Synod. So that the actual assets of the Institution may be stated, as its real estate, buildings,

---

45. T. Minutes, 1835-70, p. 142.

library, apparatus and endowment for three Professorships. This is a very different state of things from what has heretofore marked the history of the College. And we have occasion to exercise sincere and humble gratitude to God, "Who hath done great things for us whereof we are glad."[46]

---

46. Stacy, *Presbyterian Church in Georgia,* 121-122.

CHAPTER III

The University at Work

THOSE who would enter Oglethorpe University had to pass an examination on Caesar's *Commentaries,* Cicero's *Orations,* Virgil, the Gospels of the Greek Testament, Dalzel's *Collectanea, Graeca Minora,* as well as Latin and Greek grammar, arithmetic, and geography. No transcripts from secondary schools were recognized; all had to be examined in the presence of the faculty at commencement time or at the beginning of the school year.[1] Transfers from other colleges were required to "produce a certificate from the proper authority of his regular and honorable dismission and standing." But no applicant could be admitted except by a vote of the faculty.[2]

It was further provided: "Every student before he is admitted to an actual standing in any class, shall obtain from the Treasurer of the College receipts; by which it shall appear that he has complied with the existing orders of the Trustees in regard to expenses, which receipts he shall produce to an officer of the College who has at that time the instruction of the class into which he desires to enter; and if any officer admit a student to the recitations of his class, without receipts, such officer shall be responsible to the Treasurer for the expenses of such student; and this rule shall also be observed in regard to every student at the commencement of every new session of College."[3]

The school calendar never followed the unbending rules of entrance requirements. In the early history of the University, the school year was divided into two sessions. The winter session,

---

1. T. Minutes, 1835-70, p. 22; *Southern Recorder,* June 23, 1846; *Catalogue of the Officers and Students of Oglethorpe University,* 1852, p. 10.
2. T. Minutes, 1835-70, pp. 22-23.
3. *Ibid.,* 22; *Southern Recorder,* Dec. 11, 1837; April 17, 1838.

which began the collegiate year, opened on the first Monday in January, and closed the second or third Wednesday in May. The summer session began four weeks after the latter date, and closed on Commencement Day, which was the last Wednesday in October.[4] Soon commencement was changed to the Wednesday following the second Monday in November.[5]

In 1853 it was moved back to the Wednesday following the third Monday in July.[6] After this later date the school year was divided into three terms. The first term began the first week in October and ended with the Christmas holidays. The second term continued from the first Tuesday in January until the end of March, which was followed by a short spring vacation. The last term began about April 10 and ended with the July commencement exercises.[7]

Up until 1853 the first semester, which ended the second Wednesday in May, was followed by a month's vacation. This vacation was preceded by "Little Commencement," known as the May exercises, which was a source of great interest and entertainment to the people of Midway and Milledgeville.[8] From the first year of the school's operation, the local papers gave notice of them,[9] and within a few years the complete programs were published. The exercises were held in the chapel in Central Hall after its completion, and were attended by large crowds. One poetic lady who attended in 1843 related that when she rose "to depart after the solemn benediction by the President," she "could only suppress a sigh of regret by anticipating a visit to that delightful village at the close of another session, when at even a more brilliant commencement, we hope again to enjoy,—

'The feast of reason and the flow of soul.' "[10]

4. *Southern Recorder*, Dec. 11, 1837; April 17, 1838; June 23, 1846.
5. *Ibid.*, Oct. 20, 1840; Richards, ed., *Georgia Illustrated*, 8; White, *Statistics of Georgia*, 78; T. Minutes, 1835-70, p. 50.
6. *American Almanac*, 1854, p. 191; *Southern Recorder*, July 12, 1853.
7. *Southern Recorder*, July 13, 1860; *Oglethorpe University Catalogue*, 1857-58, p. 10.
8. *Southern Recorder*, May 16, 1843.
9. *Ibid.*, April 17, 1838.
.0. *Ibid.*, May 16, 1843.

A copy of the program[11] that she attended is reproduced below:

Complete Program

PRAYER BY THE PRESIDENT

MUSIC

John C. Daniel, Milledgeville,	*Woman*
G. R. Ramsey, Midway,	*The Learned Professions*

MUSIC

T. H. King, Macon,	*Past Glories of America*
James T. Nisbet, Macon,	*Indian Character*

MUSIC

W. Ivey, jr., Russell Co., Ala.	*This Government must fall*
C. E. Nisbet, Macon,	*This Government must stand*

MUSIC

H. Safford, Oglethorpe Co., Ga.	*Columbus*
T. R. Tucker, Midway,	*Memory of the Dead*

Benediction

MUSIC

Tuition varied little in the ante bellum years. At first it was $25.00 a semester, but in 1852 it was raised to $20.00 per term or $60.00 per year. Rooms were $5.00 per term. Fuel and lights were estimated at $12.00 per year. Each student was required to furnish his own room. Servant's hire was 75 cents per month. Late registrants who entered after the commencement of a session were required to pay for the whole term; those who entered after the middle of the session paid full tuition, but only half of the other expenses.[12]

---

11. It is taken from the *Southern Recorder*, May 16, 1843.
12. *Southern Recorder*, Nov. 12, 1839; June 23, 1846; *Oglethorpe University Catalogue*, 1852, pp. 11-12.

When the college opened in 1838, all students were expected to live in the twelve wooden dormitories that flanked Central Hall. As the number of students increased, some of them lived in the homes of the professors or in boarding houses. The crowded living conditions were somewhat relieved in 1859 when Thalian Hall was erected. After the completion of the Midway hotel, a few students lived there. The cost of board was from $7.00 to $10.00 per month.[13]

In the early history of the University, Oglethorpe students had to go to the wicked city of Milledgeville for their mail, as there was no post office at Midway. The faculty observed that whenever the state legislature was in session, the college boys always became seriously encumbered with weighty correspondence, and their requests for visits to the Milledgeville post office were abnormally frequent. To save the young men from going so far and so often to the worldly capital city, and to lighten their heavy load of mail, Dr. Talmage secured a post office at Midway.

New difficulties immediately arose. At that time there were fifteen villages named *Midway* in the United States; and in Georgia alone there were two: one in Baldwin County and one in Liberty County, besides a post village named *Midville* in another county. The resulting confusion was interminable. So the president of the University presented the grievance to the Post Master General of the United States and to his surprise the name of the local post office was changed to *Talmage*. This only increased the difficulty, for there were four other places in the United States with the same name (though some were spelled slightly different). As the college community was still called Midway and so written on the maps, careless correspondents persisted in addressing their letters to "Midway" as before. Mail addressed to *Talmage* often went to one of the other post offices by that name. Wherefore, strange to say, the young gentlemen of the University, with sufficient perplexity aside from postal troubles in climbing the rugged hill to knowledge, preferred to risk the vice and sin of the state capital

13. *Southern Recorder*, Nov. 6, 1838; Jacobs, *The Oglethorpe Story*, 33; Milton H. Northrup, "Recollections and Letters of Sidney Lanier," *Lippincott's Magazine*, LXXV (March, 1905), 303.

and to conduct their increasingly necessary and extensive correspondence through the Milledgeville post office—especially during the sittings of the legislature.[14]

When the University was founded, the Trustees provided that no student should enter the freshman class until he had completed his fifteenth year. The rule was not rigidly enforced, as some were allowed to enroll when they were only fourteen. To be admitted to advanced standing, students must have attained "a proportional increase of age."[15]

The long lists of rules governing the students' conduct might seem to indicate that discipline was a major problem at Oglethorpe. "All fighting, striking, quarrelling, challenging, turbulent words of behavior, profane language, violation of Sabbath shall be regarded as high offenses." Furthermore, "no firearms, sword canes, dirks, or any deadly weapon shall be allowed to be used or kept about the College."[16] In spite of these rules fights occurred occasionally. On one occasion Sidney Lanier, upon being misunderstood by a fellow student, was denounced as a liar. Immediately Lanier struck him. The student who had provoked the attack pulled his knife and stabbed his assailant in the left side. Fortunately the wound was not deep, and Lanier was able to resume his college work within two weeks.[17]

Naturally students would fight among themselves, but for fear that their pugnacious instincts might go further, the college laws solemnly warned: "Every student shall pay the utmost reverence, obedience, and respect to the person and authority of the faculty." Apparently this rule was carefully observed, for there seems to be no record in the history of Oglethorpe of a student

---

14. *Federal Union*, Aug. 23, 1871.
15. T. Minutes, 1835-70, p. 22. Sidney Lanier was 14 when he entered. Edwin Mims, *Sidney Lanier* (Boston and New York, 1905), 26.
16. T. Minutes, 1835-70, p. 26. The present writer believes discipline was no more serious problem at Oglethorpe than at other Southern colleges. See Coulter, *College Life*, 77-115. The T. Minutes, 1835-70, do not mention a single individual case of college discipline coming to the attention of that body.
17. J. O. Varnedoe, "Sidney Lanier: An Appreciation," *Georgia Historical Quarterly*, II (Sept., 1918), 139-144.

striking a faculty member. Students were admonished "to treat each other with uniform respect and kindness."[18]

The students' social life was guided by rigid regulations. "No student shall be permitted to attend any places of fashionable amusement such as theatres, horse races, or dancing assemblies during term time." Students were strictly forbidden "playing at billiards, cards; or dice or any other unlawful game for a wager." They should not keep a horse or carriage, nor were they allowed to hire one during the school session without permission of the faculty. During hours of relaxation they should not go more than one mile from the college. That students might not enjoy the conviviality engendered by intoxicants, they were not allowed to bring liquors into the college, or even to use them elsewhere.[19]

Even in his room the student's every act was regulated by meticulous rules. Upon entering college, he was assigned quarters and "in no case" was allowed to make a change without express permission of the faculty. The professors and tutors made daily visits to the rooms of the students and noted delinquents, who were reported to the faculty for discipline. All officers of the college had the right to enter the students' rooms at their pleasure. If a student resisted, the officer had the authority to break open the door, and even to require other students to assist him. Each dormitory room was inspected monthly, and all damages noted were assessed to the occupant. Damages done to the other college buildings were charged to the entire student body or to any portion of them found guilty.[20]

That which was nursed and guarded with the greatest care was the students' religion. By precept and example the faculty were required to display "an exemplary regard to moral and religious duties." It was the special duty of the president "to see that prayers are made with the students morning and evening and that religious worship is celebrated with them on the Lords [*sic*] day." During these services students should "behave with gravity and

---

18. T. Minutes, 1835-70, p. 26.
19. *Ibid.*, 25-27.
20. *Ibid.*, 21, 27, 29.

reverence." The Sabbath was holy and made for rest; hence students should not visit or receive visits or go beyond the college campus unless with express permission. On that day they should attend not only religious worship, but also a Bible recitation. Monitors were appointed by the faculty "to note down" the names of those absent from religious exercises. Absentees were reported to the faculty for discipline.[21]

For the first few years of its history, the University had a small wooden chapel, which was used until 1840. In that year, when Central Hall was completed, it was converted into recitation rooms. At the time of its completion, Central Hall was said to contain "the finest chapel in the United States."[22] It was probably one of the largest. As noted earlier, it was forty-eight by sixty feet in the main floor and seventy-one feet in the gallery, the latter extending over an eleven foot vestibule. The interior was richly decorated, and was widely noted for its beauty and elegance.

Although not instructed in Presbyterian dogma, the students were subjected to a Christian influence both broad and profound. The pious atmosphere created by the Oglethorpe faculty was, as Dr. Henry N. Snyder points out, "one which no impressionable young man could breathe for three years and afterwards depart far from its fundamental religious ideals."[23] That which did most to make converts of the students was the annual revivals. Of them a graduate of the University who became a Presbyterian minister wrote: "The crowning glory of the Institution, was the frequent outpourings of the Spirit, and precious seasons of grace. Year after year these seasons returned with almost unvarying constancy, thus in an eminent degree betokening the Divine favor."[24]

Under this pervasive atmosphere of Calvinistic piety many students joined the Presbyterian Church, as did Sidney Lanier

21. *Ibid.*, 19, 20, 25, 26.
22. Richards, ed., *Georgia Illustrated*, 7.
23. Henry Nelson Snyder, *Modern Poets and Christian Teaching: Sidney Lanier* (Cincinnati, 1906), 14.
24. Stacy, *Presbyterian Church in Georgia*, 140.

in his junior year. It is significant of Oglethorpe's religious fervor that out of three hundred and seventeen graduates, nearly one hundred became Christian ministers. Besides the graduates many matriculates entered the ministry.[25]

During all of the ante bellum period the University stuck rigidly to the beaten track of the classics. As previously noted, entrance examinations were based largely on Latin and Greek authors. The freshmen were required to read in Latin Cicero's *De Senectute, De Officiis,* and Horace's *Odes.* They read the Greek authors, Xenophon, Herodotus, and Thucydides. As though these were not enough ancient literature, they studied Roman antiquities and Latin and Greek composition. The sophomores took a like amount of Latin and Greek, but juniors and seniors were required to take only one course in the classics each semester.[26]

The undue emphasis put on the classics did not crowd out the study of science. When the University was founded, one of its Trustees proposed that in organizing the faculty there should be a professorship embracing instruction in geology, mineralogy, and botany.[27] This proposal was not immediately carried out but in 1838, when Oglethorpe began instruction, the curriculum provided for a course in astronomy, which was attached to the department of mathematics and taught by Professor Crawford. As noted earlier, in 1839 Professor Howard purchased $1,500 worth of scientific apparatus in Europe. The next year a course was begun in natural philosophy, which included all the sciences except astronomy. After a few years chemistry was added to the curriculum.[28] In 1851 the Trustees elected to the chair of chemical geology and natural history, Dr. Joseph Le Conte, a young scientist,[29] who was to become one of America's most noted geologists.

A native Georgian, Professor Le Conte was graduated from the

25. *Ibid.;* Varnedoe, *loc. cit.,* 140; *Southern Recorder,* July 28, 1868.
26. T. Minutes, 1835-70, pp. 23-24; *Oglethorpe University Catalogue,* 1852, pp. 11-12; *ibid.,* 1857, pp. 12-14.
27. T. Minutes, 1835-70, p. 11.
28. *Ibid.,* 36, 37, 42, 54.
29. *Ibid.,* 141; William Dallam Armes, ed., *The Autobiography of Joseph Le Conte* (New York, 1903), 154.

State University in 1841, and after studying medicine at the College of Physicians and Surgeons in New York City, he was awarded the degree of Doctor of Medicine in 1845. After spending a year traveling and observing nature at first hand in the sparsely settled Northwest, he returned to Georgia and practiced medicine in Macon. He found the life of a general practitioner very distasteful, and after a few years gave it up to go to Harvard to study under the noted Louis Agassiz. His association with Agassiz was most intimate, and in January, 1851, he accompanied him on a scientific expedition to the reefs of Florida. After graduation from Harvard's Lawrence Scientific School, Le Conte came back to Georgia and was elected to teach at Oglethorpe in November, 1851. He began his work in January, 1852.[30]

Dr. Le Conte taught mechanics, physics, chemistry, geology, and botany. This full schedule occupied all of his time, but, as he later wrote, "This was excellent training for me, for it kept alive my interest in all departments of science, which is especially necessary in geology, which was to become my chief study." Far in advance of his day, Dr. Le Conte used modern scientific methods in his teaching, though he was handicapped by want of satisfactory textbooks, except in botany. In this course he used Gray's *Structural and Physiological Botany*. For the laboratory he gathered native plants and dissected them. He was materially aided by "a first-rate microscope."[31]

Dr. Le Conte was succeeded by Dr. James Woodrow, a maternal uncle of President Woodrow Wilson. Born in Carlisle, England, in 1828, he had been brought to the United States when he was nine years old. His father settled in Chillicothe, Ohio, where the boy grew up, but he attended Jefferson College, in Canonsburg, Pennsylvania, where he was graduated with highest honors in 1849. After teaching in several academies in Alabama, he was elected professor of natural science at Oglethorpe. Professor Woodrow taught until the summer of 1853, when he was granted a leave of absence to do graduate work at Harvard under Agassiz, as his predecessor had done. From Harvard, Woodrow

---

30. Armes, ed., *The Autobiography of Joseph Le Conte*, 54, 62-64, 127-154.
31. *Ibid.*, 155.

went to Heidelberg, where he took the Ph.D., *summa cum laude.*
He is said to have been offered a full professorship at Heidelberg,
but he declined and returned to Oglethorpe in 1856.[32]

As a professor of science, he became the ornament of the faculty. He was the first teacher in the history of Georgia to hold
a Ph.D. degree.[33] In long retrospect one of his admiring students
wrote: "Professor Woodrow possessed the finest general scholarship and could have filled with ability any chair in the college,
but he was especially accomplished as a scientist. His instructions
were highly valued . . . . "[34] Late in life Sidney Lanier called him
"the strongest and most valuable stimulus" of his youth. He added:
"I am more indebted to Dr. Woodrow than to any living man,
for shaping my mental attitude toward nature and life. His spirit
and method had a formative influence on my thought and fancy
in all my literary work."[35]

While Dr. Woodrow was teaching at Oglethorpe, Darwin published his *On the Origin of Species* (London, 1859). Dr. Woodrow
accepted Darwin's thesis and taught the theory of evolution
because he believed its truth. He maintained firmly and persistently that evolution was God's plan of creation. He explained,
"God's work and God's word cannot contradict each other."[36]

Dr. Woodrow's ideas on evolution, which were published in
the July, 1884, issue of the *Southern Presbyterian Review*, pre-
cipitated a widespread controversy that led to his demanding a
trial by his Presbytery. Though he was declared "not guilty,"
he was forced to resign his professorship in the Columbia Theological Seminary, to which he had gone from Oglethorpe in 1861. In
1888 he was tried for heresy before the General Assembly of the
Southern Presbyterian Church and was condemned as a heretic,
though he persistently avowed his full belief in the Bible and his

32. Marion W. Woodrow, ed., *Dr. James Woodrow: Character Sketches and
    Teachings* (Columbia, S. C., 1909), 8-12; *Who's Who in America*, 1906-
    1907.
33. This statement is based on a careful checking of the extant catalogues
    of professors in all Georgia colleges before 1856.
34. E. M. Green in Jacobs, ed., *The Oglethorpe Story*, 97 n.
35. Quoted in Woodrow, *Dr. James Woodrow*, 12.
36. Ray Stannard Baker, *Woodrow Wilson: Life and Letters* (8 vols., New
    York, 1927-35), I, 21-22.

acceptance of the Presbyterian creed. For Dr. Woodrow there was never any conflict between science and theology.[37] He represented "modern academic thought at its best, liberal and tolerant; what he as a teacher most desired was to develop in young men a sense of responsibility for their own opinions and a capacity to form them intelligently."[38] To his students he opened a new world of scientific speculation and revealed the meaning of genuine scholarship.

To attain high standards of scholarship various methods were used by other members of the faculty. While Dr. Woodrow and Dr. Le Conte used chiefly the lecture method, oral questioning seems to have been used more generally. Students of Greek and Latin were assigned a given number of lines to read daily, which they translated in class. Parsing was an essential part of the recitation.[39] The freshmen and sophomores had four classes a day, while upper classmen had only three.[40] The day began with morning prayers, followed by recitations and study periods that lasted until sundown. This busy schedule was ended by vesper services, after which the students went to their rooms and prepared the next day's assignments. In the middle of the day there was a lunch period that lasted two hours. There were strict rules governing attendance at classes and religious services, and woe to the student who was absent without a good excuse![41]

Before the University opened its doors, it had been realized that a library was necessary for the promotion of knowledge. The few students that entered Oglethorpe on January 1, 1838, found three hundred books in the college library.[42] Before the end of the year an advertisement appeared in the Milledgeville *Southern Recorder* soliciting "the friends of literature and of the Institution donations of books." A committee, composed of members from various parts of the state, and headed by Joseph Henry Lumpkin,

---

37. *Ibid.*, 22, 209-210. See also P. E. Graham, "James Woodrow, Calvinist and Evolutionist," *Sewanee Review*, XL (July-Sept., 1932), 307-315.
38. Starke, *Sidney Lanier*, 32-33.
39. Cf. Mims, *Sidney Lanier*, 30; Jacobs, *The Oglethorpe Story*, 98 n. See also *Oglethorpe University Catalogue*, 1857, p. 10.
40. *Oglethorpe University Catalogue*, 1852, p. 5; *ibid.*, 1857, p. 5.
41. T. Minutes, 1835-70, pp. 20, 25-26.
42. *Ibid.*, 38.

was named to receive contributions.[43] Apparently the committee was highly successful, for six years later the University reported two thousand volumes in its library.[44] Each of the two literary societies—the Thalians and Phi Deltas—had its own library which together, in 1860, contained probably one thousand volumes.[45] By that time the University library had grown to four thousand five hundred books, making a total of fifty-five hundred. As compared with other colleges in Georgia and the nation, that number was more than average.[46]

The library was never large enough to have a building of its own; neither did it have a full time librarian.[47] It was kept in a room in Central Hall and was composed largely of theological books, translations of the classics, and English and American authors. There were no magazines or newspapers and few novels, as these were considered improper literature by puritanical Presbyterians.[48] For a few students, at least, the library was the most popular department of the college. One student has left a list of some of the books that he read in his junior year:[49]

Robert Burton's *Anatomy of Melancholy*
Jeremy Taylor's *The Poet Preacher*
Keats' *Endymion* and *Chatterton*
North's *Noctes Ambrosianae*
Tennyson's "Locksley Hall," "In Memoriam," and "Maud"
Carlyle's *Sartor Resartus, Hero Worship,* and *Past and Present*

Doubtless Sidney Lanier found his happiest and most profitable hours reading in the library. While he was a student at Oglethorpe,

43. Dec. 11, 1838.
44. *American Almanac,* 1844, p. 189.
45. Minutes of the Thalian Society, 1859-1863, of Oglethorpe University, *passim.* This manuscript, which was found by Mrs. Leola Beeson, is in the Library of the Georgia State College for Women, Milledgeville.
46. *American Almanac,* 1860, pp. 204-205.
47. In 1859-60 S. L. Knox was tutor and librarian. *Southern Recorder,* Sept. 13, 1860.
48. George Barnsley, "Recollections of Oglethorpe University, Midway, Ga.— 1854-1857," p. 2. In the George Barnsley Papers, Southern Historical Collection, University of North Carolina Library, Chapel Hill.
49. T. F. Newell in W. M. Baskervill, *Southern Writers: Biographical and Critical Studies* (Nashville, 1899), I, 149-150, 154-155.

his literary talents first began to be evidenced, and a study of his college reading shows its influence in his later writings.[50] It is worthy of note that, besides Lanier, who became Georgia's greatest poet, Oglethorpe furnished the state several other literary talents of distinction: Clifford Lanier, Isaac W. Avery, and Joseph M. Brown.

More generally popular with the student body than the library was the art of orating. The faculty required two students from the lower classes to speak every evening at vespers, and juniors and seniors were required to deliver orations of their own composition at least once a month. On the Fourth of July the whole day was given to patriotic addresses. All of Saturdays was consumed by "forensic disputations" in the literary societies. At commencement there were usually three whole days of orating and declaiming.[51]

In spite of their full daily routine, Oglethorpe students found time for relaxation and merry making. With some the gymnasium was popular.[52] Others found entertainment in music and song. "I shall never forget," recalled one of Sidney Lanier's roommates, "those moonlight nights at old Oglethorpe, when, after study, we would crash up the stairway and get out on the cupola, making the night merry with music, song, and laughter. Sid would play on his flute like one inspired, while the rest of us would listen in solemn silence"[53] The music was so clear and sweet that it could be heard two miles away in Milledgeville. Soon Lanier, with his flute, William Le Conte, with his violin, and John Lamar, with his violoncello, formed a small orchestra that furnished the student "exquisitely beautiful music."[54] Occasionally a group of the boys would serenade the young ladies of Midway and Milledgeville. Dr. Talmage, strict Calvinist though he was, gave the musicians his "official warrant to practice their art among the townspeople." "The music was satisfactory enough," reported Le Conte, "to lead the different households to look forward with pleasant

50. Starke, *Sidney Lanier*, 27-28; Mims, *Sidney Lanier*, 34.
51. T. Minutes, 1835-70, p. 24; and *infra* Chapters IV and VI.
52. Varnedoe, *loc. cit.*, 139.
53. *Ibid.;* T. F. Newell, *loc. cit.*, 149.
54. Jacobs, *The Oglethorpe Story*, 35 n, 98 n.

anticipation to our return and often to show their appreciation by a market basket, let down by a rope from some balcony or window from above and containing choice viands, which were fully enjoyed by us boys, accustomed to boarding house fare."[55]

On one occasion things went wrong for the troubadours, and they laughed at themselves. One of them related: "I recall on one very cold winter night when the serenading party, with benumbed fingers, had performed the three or four conventional tunes of the serenade at the house of General Lamar, whose daughter was one of the local belles, that the gray-haired butler appeared at the door, not to invite the chilled troubadours into a warm parlor for refreshments, but to announce that 'Marsa an' de young ladies done been down to de plantation 'bout a week.' "[56]

Sometimes the University sponsored special programs that were both entertaining and educational. In 1847 noted speakers from various parts of the state gave a series of lectures on the following subjects: "Anatomy," "Application of Chemistry to Agriculture," "Geology," "International Law," "Natural Science," and "Political Science." The lectures were given in the Chapel at Midway, and the public was invited. Crowds from Midway and Milledgeville attended.[57]

On rare occasions the professors would accompany a group of students to Milledgeville to hear a noted speaker at the State Capitol. On the evening of November 15, 1860, Benjamin H. Hill addressed the state legislature on secession. Chaperoned by Dr. Talmage and Mr. Lane, some of the Oglethorpe students went to hear the address. Both of the professors cautioned the students against making any demonstration at all.

Ben Hill spoke for two hours and gave powerful arguments against secession. The two professors approved of Hill's address so heartily they almost forgot their admonitions to the students. Dr. Talmage had a habit of rubbing his hands together when he was especially pleased, and Professor Lane, of nodding his head

---

55. Lincoln Lorenz, *The Life of Sidney Lanier* (New York, 1935), 17-18.
56. Henry W. Lanier, ed., *Selections from Sidney Lanier, Prose and Verse* (New York, Chicago, and Boston, 1916), xi.
57. *Southern Recorder*, June 23, 1946; and *passim*.

to express his approbation. Afterwards the boys told that Dr. Talmage rubbed the skin off his hands and Professor Lane had a stiff neck for two weeks afterwards.[58]

As a rule there were cordial relations between the faculty and students. A congenial and affectionate intimacy often arose between them. As noted above, Sidney Lanier had a deep admiration for Professor Woodrow. Sometimes they strolled through the woods together, as the Professor later wrote, "observing and studying whatever we saw, but also talking about everything either of us cared for." Occasionally Lanier would accompany his mentor on long drives to his preaching appointments. "During such drives," recalled Professor Woodrow, "we were constantly engaged without interruption in our conversation. In these ways, and in listening frequently to his marvelous flute-playing, we were much together. We were both young and fond of study."[59]

A student of Professor Charles W. Lane, head of the mathematics department, remembered him, in long retrospect, as "a man of great simplicity of character, 'an Israelite in whom was no guile.' He was universally esteemed for his goodness and was an excellent and faithful teacher."[60] Another wrote of him that he was "the sunniest, sweetest Calvinist that ever nestled close to the heart of Arminians and all else who loved the Master's image when they saw it. His cottage at Midway was a Bethel; it was God's house and Heaven's gate."[61]

58. Beeson, *Sidney Lanier at Oglethorpe*, 30; *Southern Recorder*, Nov. 20, 1860.
59. Mims, *Sidney Lanier*, 30.
60. Jacobs, *The Oglethorpe Story*, 92 n.
61. Mims, *Sidney Lanier*, 27-28.

CHAPTER IV

Thalians and Phi Deltas

OGLETHORPE University was just a year old when a group of students met in January, 1839, to organize a secret society for the promotion of oratory, declamation, debating, and other literary pursuits.[1] They named their new organization Thalia in honor of "the father of philosophy" who introduced metaphysics into ancient Greece and found the origin of all things in water. As Thales sought to discover the origin of the universe, so his followers at Oglethorpe tried to solve all its problems. They wanted to be philosophers like this wise old Greek and naturally looked to him for precept and example; they studied his life and teachings and held him up as their guide and mentor. To show the world that they were his disciples, they proudly wore a large gold emblem of the size of a half dollar. On its top was engraved THALIA and on the bottom the Greek symbols for Theta Tau Sigma. It was to be worn as a watch fob or pinned on the lapel of the coat. On special occasions, such as commencement or the Fourth of July, it was put on a silken badge to make it more conspicuous.[2]

Like all philosophers, the Thalians were never so happy as when they were disputing some point of logic or arguing the evils of the human race. Herein lay the seeds of dissension and its companions— rivalry and finally secession. Thalia was not two years old when a new society was born. Its object was "to teach its members how to give utterance to their thoughts, to debate, to speak in public with ease and grace."[3] The new society called itself Phi Delta in

1. *Catalogue of the Thalian Literary Society of Oglethorpe University* (Charleston, S. C., 1858), 3.
2. One of the emblems is in the History Room of the library at the Georgia State College for Women in Milledgeville.
3. George S. Barnsley, "Farewell Address to the Phi Delta Society of Oglethorpe University," a manuscript in the George S. Barnsley Papers, Southern Historical Collection, University of North Carolina Library, Chapel Hill. Phi Delta is first mentioned in the *Southern Recorder*, Nov. 17, 1840.

public, but these Greek letters stood for Greek words meaning "lover of reasoning," and were unknown to all except the initiated.[4] The Phi Deltas selected for their emblem a neat little gold pin inscribed with the Latin motto LUX ET VIRTUS ("Light and Virtue"). Just above the motto there appeared a tiny square and compasses—the symbol of VIRTUS—which was to remind its wearer that he was to square his actions and to keep them in due bounds.[5] In the middle of the emblem was an altar on which was a burning fire—the symbol of LUX, the light of religion and truth. On the left of the altar was a quill, which denoted the literary objectives of the society. On the right was a key—the key to knowledge, which every Phi Delta must seek.[6]

From the first there was intense if not friendly rivalry between the Thalians and Phi Deltas. For every class honor and every prize offered by the University each society vied with enthusiasm and determination to win over the other. At the beginning of the school year each tried to secure as many new members as possible from the incoming students. The one seems to have been about as successful as the other in pledging neophytes, for always at commencement and other public meetings approximately the same number represented each society. On such occasions the printed programs and newspaper accounts recorded for public notice each contestant's literary affiliation so every one could judge the comparative excellence of Thalians and Phi Deltas. A major ambition of most members was to win a class medal or to be an honor graduate. Those receiving prizes were highly esteemed by their fellow literarians, and their achievements were never forgotten. The names of the honor graduates were recorded with distinguishing marks in catalogues that were published and widely distributed among the students, the faculty, and the friends of Oglethorpe.

At commencement in July, 1857, a departing senior, in his

---

4. Cf. Minutes of Phi Delta Literary Society, 1834-1915, p. 10. These minutes are in the Mercer University Library, in Macon, Georgia.
5. Cf. Albert G. Mackey, *An Encyclopaedia of Freemasonry* (2 vols., Chicago, New York, and London, 1921), II, 708.
6. Miss Betty Ferguson, reference librarian, of G.S.C.W., lent her grandfather's, William Alexander Williams's, emblem for this description.

"Farewell Address to the Phi Delta Society," warned: "It is particularly necessary at this time that each and every member of the Society should faithfully discharge his duties. The crisis now has come. The Thalian Society now equals us in number. Already we hear their hurrahs at their success in numbers—already we perceive their sneers and their jests, arising from a foolish pride founded upon their increase in numbers. Long did they, while few in number, give utterance to the boast that 'Though few in numbers yet they surpass in talent.' - But have they shown that the boast is true? Who took the first prize in the Sophomore Exhibition of 1855? A Phi Delta. - Who took all the prizes three in number in 1856? P. Ds. Who were the best men of the classes of '55 and '56? Phi Deltas. Who, I ask again, have carried off their share [of] honors in the present class? P. D.'s. once more. Does this show that they surpass us in talent? In all strifes whether in the chapel or in the recitation room P. D. has never sunk below excellence, while often she has risen superior. It is the greatest aim and the 'ultima Thule' of Thalia's honored sons to equal Phi Delta's children. Long and nobly have P. D.'s. sons held the vantage ground, and never to my recollection has she been worsted. - But, loved comrades, be not puffed up. The enemy is on the alert. They are straining every sinew - every nerve, to equal and to eventually surpass us. Every year the battle rages more fiercely. In the contest soon to come off nobly stand your ground. Struggle once more to plant Phi Delta's triumphant standard upon the heights of glory. Be diligent, be watchful, be guarded in your actions in and out of the Hall. Be it your pride that no Phi Delta shall ever leave this seat of learning in disgrace."[7]

In nothing that the Thalians and Phi Deltas did was the competitive spirit keener than in their constantly striving to increase their numbers by electing honorary members. The surviving minutes of the Thalians show that at almost every regular meeting one or more Southerners of note, if not of fame, were elected. Among those so honored were Governor M. A. Perry, of Florida; John Bell, of Tennessee; the poet Henry Jackson, of Savannah; and Dr. John Le Conte, then of Philadelphia, but originally from

---

7. George Barnsley, "Farewell Address to the Phi Delta Society."

Georgia.[8] Once a noted scientist was elected, but in accepting
the honor he reported he was already a Phi Delta. Immediately
it was decided that henceforth honorary membership would be
conferred only on those who stated that they did not belong to
the rival society.[9] The Phi Deltas were equally as zealous in scour-
ing the South for honorary members. In fact, the few surviving
records of Phi Delta included the names of more famous Southerners than the list of honorary Thalians: Herschel V. Johnson,
soon to be Vice-Presidential candidate with Stephen Douglas in
1860;[10] John B. Gordon, destined to Confederate fame;[11] and Dr.
Joseph Le Conte, to become a greater scientist than his brother
John who was an honorary Thalian.[12]

At first, each society met in a room in Central Hall designated
by the faculty,[13] but in 1854 it was decided to erect separate and
independent halls on the scholarship plan. The Phi Deltas set
to work at once to raise the $1,500 required by the faculty before
beginning construction and sent a form letter to "their friends and
the friends of the University and of Education," soliciting them
to contribute to the cost of erecting "such an edifice as will com-
port with the dignity and increasing importance of the University."[14] Apparently the Phi Deltas met with little success as their
hall was never erected.[15]

If the Thalians got a later start, they met with better fortune
than their rival society. Construction of their hall was begun in
1859, but it required nearly two years for its completion and in-
volved the society in countless difficulties. Once the Thalians were
informed that unless they paid the building committee the necessary
$1,500, the faculty would offer the new hall to the Phi Deltas, and

---

8. Thalian Minutes, 1, 29, 77.
9. *Ibid.*, 31, 37, 41.
10. Herschel V. Johnson, *Obligations of Civilization to the Arts and Science* (Milledgeville, Georgia, 1856), 1.
11. John B. Gordon, *Progress of Civil Liberty* (Macon, Ga., 1861), 1.
12. Thalian Minutes, 31.
13. Barnsley, "Recollections of Old Oglethorpe," 2.
14. I. W. Avery to W. Cleveland. This copy of the letter is in the American Antiquarian Society Library at Worcester, Mass. It is dated June 19, 1854.
15. Cf. Beeson, *Sidney Lanier*, 17.

JOSEPH LE CONTE
From a portrait by Scarbrough

JOHN LE CONTE
From a photograph owned by the
University of California Library

WILLIAM JACOB SASNETT
From a portrait at Emory University

if the latter did not take it, it would be converted into dormitories.[16] On another occasion the Thalians refused to pay the $1,500 assessment until the faculty delivered the hall into their hands in a finished condition.[17] Finally after several months of wrangling and discussions, the hall was completed and the society moved in on January 12, 1861.[18]

The structure, which still stands, is of plain red brick and three stories in height. It is 82 feet long and 48 feet wide. The first and second stories are each divided into eight rooms and were used by the Thalians as a dormitory. Each room has a fireplace. The third story was one long hall and was used by the society for its meetings and social affairs.

The Thalians were proud of their new hall and made every effort to provide for its care and upkeep. Soon after its occupancy, a motion was carried that "the members be not allowed to smoke in the Hall on Saturday morning" and "A motion prevailed that the Committee on Arrangements be instructed to buy twenty spittoons," which of course was to save the new carpet from tobacco juice. Any member who should be so careless as to soil the floor was subject to a twenty-five cent fine. The same amount was assessed for "taking the cushions out of the chairs, and laying them on the floor."[19]

There were no classes on Saturday, and the whole day was given over to literary pursuits. Every student was expected to join one of the societies, and anyone who had so little interest in literary affairs as not to join a society was restricted. As a result there were few who did not become Thalians or Phi Deltas. The societies put special emphasis upon attendance. Every meeting was opened with a roll call, and woe unto the member who was absent without a good excuse! The usual penalty was a fine, but continued absences might result in expulsion.[20]

There were the usual officers to be found in societies in general, but several others besides: President, Vice-President, Record-

---

16. Thalian Minutes, 69.
17. *Ibid.*, 65.
18. *Ibid.*, 63, 69. See also Beeson, *Sidney Lanier*, 20.
19. *Ibid.*, 93, 125, 131, 148.
20. *Ibid.*, *passim*.

ing Secretary, Corresponding Secretary, First Librarian, Second Librarian, Chaperon, Treasurer, Solicitor, Assistant Solicitor, First Judge, and Second Judge. The presidency was naturally the highest office and was aspired to by all the ambitious. Like a chief executive, the president delivered an inaugural address. On December 10, 1859, when Sidney Lanier became president of the Thalians, it was recorded that "the ex-president conducted his successor to the chair who made an eloquent and interesting address. The new Officers took their seats. Speeches were made by new Officers in obedience to calls."[21] Like the ancient Romans the officers donned the *toga virilis*—a sort of long purple dressing gown— when they took their seats.[22]

The societies began at 8 o'clock in the morning. The hour of adjournment was indefinite, as the orations and debates sometimes lasted until noon. If at that time the arguments were not concluded, a recess was ordered until after "dinner." At 2 p.m. the debates were resumed. They were usually finished before sundown. On special occasions matters which were considered of more importance drew the Thalians and Phi Deltas to Milledgeville, the state capital. But even then, the societies had a short meeting, when it was formally decided that the regular meeting would be postponed. Besides the regular meetings often there were called meetings.[23]

The order of business in the Thalian society seems to have followed a strict pattern:

1. First roll call
2. Reading of the minutes
3. Election of honorary members
4. Election of regular members (whose names were presented by the Chaperon, balloted on, and, if elected, duly initiated)
5. Report of committees on questions
6. Arrangements
7. Special business

21. *Ibid.*, 31, 32.
22. Charles R. Anderson, ed., *Sidney Lanier* (Centennial edition, 10 vols., Baltimore, 1945), VII, 24. Hereinafter cited as *Sidney Lanier*, cent. ed.
23. Thalian Minutes, *passim*.

8. Declaimers
9. Discussion of question of last debate
10. Announcement of the decision
11. Miscellaneous business
12. Session of the Court
13. Last roll call

The last item of business was included to make sure that no member had slipped out before adjournment.[24]

At the Session of the Court, penalties were imposed upon those who had violated any of the numerous rules of the society. For minor offenses small fines were assessed, but were often repealed at the following meeting. The penalties for more serious violations ranged from heavy fines to expulsion.[25] In 1859, after a Thalian was expelled, the society voted to erase his name from the list of members, and from the catalogues, and a committee was appointed to inform him of his expulsion. Soon thereafter it was decided that thenceforth "the names of all expelled and resigned members be stricken from the catalogue." Even honorary members were subject to expulsion. In 1860 the Phi Deltas expelled a Dr. Howe, for reasons that are not clear, and his name was expunged from the roll.[26]

Debating was the chief business of the societies and consumed the major part of nearly every regular program. The college boys presented their arguments with the seriousness that is becoming older men who are members of august legislative assemblies. A characteristic comment, found in the Thalian minutes, was, "The question was read and discussed very interestingly and ably."[27] If the announced debate did not last long, a committee was appointed who repaired to the library and chose a second subject, which was argued extemporaneously at the same session. Before adjournment the question to be taken up at the next meeting was announced and debaters were chosen for each side. They were

---

24. *Ibid.*
25. *Ibid.*
26. *Ibid.*, 6, 32, 37. See also Beeson, *Sidney Lanier*, 5.
27. Thalian Minutes, 125.

expected to study the topic and to discuss it only after careful preparation.

The subjects of debate were varied and embraced chiefly history, literature, religion, and current topics, but also philosophy and logic. The questions were decided not by a committee of impartial judges but by a vote of the members or by the president. Once a Thalian complained that the president should decide the debate "by the preponderance of argument."[28] But as most questions were settled by popular vote and the results recorded, the decisions furnish a firsthand account of what Southern college boys were thinking about in the years that witnessed the disruption of the Union. An analysis of the voting, especially on current topics, indicates that the thought of the future leaders was not far ahead of that of the common masses as expressed in elections and resolutions of organized bodies such as churches and political conventions. In fact the opinions of the college students pointed a way of action to those less informed.

Thus on December 17, 1859, only two weeks after John Brown was hanged, the Thalians debated, "Does the Harper's ferry insurrection justify secession of the South?" They decided that it was not yet time to secede.[29] This view was generally held throughout the Southern states at that time, as it was still felt that this one incident hardly represented the attitude of most Northerners. But with the nomination of Lincoln in May, 1860, Southerners became more disposed to secession sentiment, and Thalians doubtless expressed that sentiment when two weeks after the Republican convention adjourned, they considered, "Would the formation of a Southern confederacy enhance the commercial prosperity of the South?" The question "was warmly discussed and decided in favor of the affirmative by a majority of ten."[30]

At the next meeting the debaters considered the question, "Should the Southern people endorse the action of the seceders [from the Democratic National Convention] at Charleston?" By

28. *Ibid.*, 15.
29. *Ibid.*, 33, 34.
30. *Ibid.*, 57, 58.

Thalian Hall.

Sidney Lanier's Room in Thalian Hall.

a majority of eight Thalians endorsed the action of these pro-
slavery Democrats and immediately began discussing their political arguments which Southerners everywhere were consider-
ing. In June, 1860, the Thalians asked, "Is the progress of the
South in literature and fine arts impeded by her institutions of
Slavery?" and they answered with a strong negative vote of
ten majority.[31] Just four weeks after Georgia withdrew from the
Union, the same question was attacked from a different angle:
"Has the advancement of the Southern States in power and wealth
been retarded by the institution of Slavery?" By a majority of
five they decided in favor of the negative, thereby accepting again
the old arguments of the slavery interests, who were now succeeding in convincing most Southerners of the justice of their
cause.[32]

The Phi Deltas shared the views of the Thalians regarding the
righteousness of slavery. At commencement in 1860 they invited
a rising young orator from northeast Alabama who had accompanied William L. Yancey on a campaign tour, speaking in behalf of John C. Breckinridge.[33] "Young Gentlemen of the Phi
Delta Society," he said, "permit me . . . to suggest to you and to
all the young gentlemen whom I have the honor to address, that
when you have left these pleasant scenes and associations to take
your positions politically among your fellowmen, you make
it your first great duty to thoroughly understand the provisions
of our constitution. Be ready to render to every section of the
Jnion its rights, under that instrument. Ask no more for the
South—submit to nothing less. And so far from admitting that
Negro slavery is an evil and an instrument of tyranny, take the
position, everywhere, that it is morally, socially, and politically
right . . . ."[34] The Phi Deltas thoroughly approved these Southern
rights doctrines, and wishing that others might have the privilege
of knowing them, they sent a committee to the speaker who
thanked him for his "able, eloquent and instructive address," and

---

31. *Ibid.*, 62, 63.
32. *Ibid.*, 91, 93.
33. *Atlanta Constitution*, Nov. 24, 1878.
34. Gordon, *Progress of Civil Liberty*, 17.

requested a copy of the manuscript for publication. Their request was granted, and copies of the address were widely distributed just at the time when the war spirit was seizing Georgia and the South.[35]

Like most Southerners of the slave holding class, both Phi Deltas and Thalians were convinced, paradoxically enough, that democratic principles were good for the rest of the world. A month after the Mexican War closed, a Phi Delta lauded John Locke's dictum, "All men are born free and equal" and rejoiced that God "is fast hastening that great political jubilee,—the triumph of equal rights throughout the world."[36] A month after the Confederate Constitution was adopted, legalizing slavery forever, the Thalians decided that England would be benefited by making her government strictly republican. Shortly before, they had asked, "Which is more conducive to the arts and literature, a monarchical or Republican form of government?" They voted overwhelmingly against monarchy.[37] They never grew tired of singing the praises of the founding fathers of the American republic—Washington, Madison, and Hamilton—and of those who fought for its freedom— La Fayette, Moultrie, Marion, and John Twiggs, "the Saviour of Georgia" in the Revolution. Yet they were chivalrous enough to say on one occasion that Major André should not have been hanged as a spy, and they thought that Southerners were not more justified in their resistance to the North than were their forefathers in that to England.[38]

In general, the Thalians were not revolutionists and believed in maintaining the established government. Doubtless it was for that reason that they decided that Brutus should not have joined the conspiracy against Julius Caesar and that the French revolutionists did not aid the cause of liberty. In like manner, they held that Oliver Cromwell was not a true patriot. They later decided by one vote that he was motived more by "enlightenment piety"

35. *Ibid.*, 3.
36. John MacNeil Smith, *An Oration delivered before the Thalian and Phi Delta Societies, of Oglethorpe University, July 4, 1848* (Milledgeville, 1848), 14.
37. Thalian Minutes, 90, 91, 99, 101.
38. *Ibid.*, 113, 115, 130, 131, and *passim*.

than by "fanaticism." But the execution of Charles I was not "justifiable." Neither was that of Mary Queen of Scots. Pagan governments, however, might be destroyed. The Thalians, by a majority of one, voted that the fall of the Ottoman Empire would benefit Europe, and by a larger vote they decided that more evil than good had resulted to the world from the life and religion of Mahomet.[39]

Besides those already mentioned, there were many other historical topics that furnished a fertile field for discussion and debate—"the glory that was Greece and the grandeur that was Rome," the right that the Indians had to the soil, the benefit to Europe that the Crusades rendered, and the wonderful achievements that made the United States great. Demosthenes, Cicero, and Caesar, of old, and Washington, Hamilton, and Henry Clay, of more recent times, thundered in the halls of Phi Deltas and Thalians. The latter inquired in 1862, "Which was the greater general, Caesar or Hannibal?" and decided in favor of the Carthaginian. A few years before, when the same question was debated by the Phi Deltas, Caesar was voted the greater. The historical interest of the Thalians swept easily from primitive man to events that had transpired in their own day. In the fall of 1859 they denied the right of savages to possess the soil, and a few months later they took up the current question, "Was the Mexican War justifiable?" and answered strongly in the affirmative, as most Southerners were then doing to justify their grab of new territory for the expansion of the slave power.[40] Both Thalians and Phi Deltas believed that Cuba should "be acquired *vi et armis*" for the same purpose.[41]

French history in general, and especially that phase dealing with the Revolution, were ever popular subjects for discussion and argument. The Thalians showed their sympathy for Louis XVI when they decided by a large majority that his execution was not "justifiable." Once they compared Washington with La Fayette

---

39. *Ibid.*, 14, 15, 42, 45, 46, 79, 83, 85, 117, 118, 119.
40. *Ibid.*, 51, 52, 82, 83, 131, 132. See also Barnsley, "Recollections of Oglethorpe University, 1854-1857," p. 20.
41. *Ibid.*, 82, 85; Gordon, *Progress of Civil Liberty*, 16.

and voted a greater measure of praise for the Marquis than for "the Father of his Country."[42] Speaking of this foreign friend of America, a Thalian said of him in a public address in the chapel: "The scorching rays of envy cannot blast—falsehood cannot destroy his fame, for it is identified with the history of him, who hath justly been pronounced the 'greatest, noblest, purest of mankind.' "[43] But to Thalians the most interesting of all Frenchmen was Napoleon. As a general they thought him more able than Alexander the Great, but felt that the banishment of the Corsican to St. Helena was proper and that his career as a whole was not worthy of admiration.[44] When a guest speaker of the Phi Deltas referred to Napoleon as a "moral monster deformed and defective" and "a misanthrope," the society wholeheartedly approved his address.[45] There were many questions to answer in the career of the "Little Corporal": "Was he justified in divorcing Josephine?" and "Was he greater in the field or in the Cabinet?" To answer these and other such problems, the Thalians purchased J. S. C. Abbot's *Napoleon Bonaparte* (New York, 1856) in two volumes and added them to their growing library.[46]

The eternal question of woman was as interesting and perplexing to Oglethorpe men as to males from Adam to modern movie actors. More than fifty years before women were admitted to any men's college in Georgia, the Thalians asked, "Are mixed [*i.e.*, coeducational] schools productive of more good than evil?" The topic was "warmly discussed" and in keeping with the standards of Southern chivalry the answer was *yes* by a majority of five. Having decided that women should attend college with men, the Thalians raised the question, "Is married life better than single life?" and voted for married life. But if this course is better than living alone, "Are early marriages preferable?" The Thalians

---

42. Thalian Minutes, 18, 19, 136, 137.
43. A. Sydney Hartridge, *An Oration Delivered before the Phi-Delta and Thalian Societies of Oglethorpe University* (Macon, 1848), 5.
44. Thalian Minutes, 65, 66, 67, 120, 130, 131.
45. Thomas Smyth, *Denominational Education . . . Address Delivered before the Thalian and Phi-Delta Societies of Oglethorpe University* (Charleston, S. C., 1846), 15.
46. Thalian Minutes, 132, 139, 149.

decided that they were *not*, but pursued the problem further: "Are early marriages conducive to the advancement of Society?" *Yes*, they answered, somewhat in contradiction to their former stand, indicating they believed that early marriages were good for society at large but not for the individual.[47]

Granting that marriage must come early for the advancement of the social order, the Thalians were anxious to protect the home. What could do this better than Christian education and religion, especially in its Protestant form, or better still according to Presbyterianism? The Phi Deltas agreed that the Presbyterian Church was "liberal and eminently adapted to be the guardian and patron of a religious education." They were tolerant of other Protestant bodies, but they condemned "the darkness of Popery" with the vehemence of a John Calvin or John Knox.[48]

The Thalians also denounced Roman Catholicism and voted that it was incompatible with free institutions. However, by the largest majority recorded, seventeen, they agreed that religious toleration was not a menace to republican institutions. Infidels were considered even more dangerous than Catholics and ought not to be allowed to testify in a court of justice. Strangely, these pious sons of pious Presbyterians had little fear of Mormonism, for in 1859 they voted that it ought not to be abolished *vi et armis*. Their tolerance of the practice of polygamy is probably best explained by the fact that many abolitionists at that time were combining their attacks against plural marriages and slavery as twin evils of barbarism.[49]

In other questions of a moral character, both Thalians and Phi Deltas displayed as much respect for Puritanism as the Presbyterians of that day. Both societies agreed with the church on the value of reading and studying the Bible. The Thalians thought that the Holy Writ ought to be adopted in the common schools as an ordinary reading book. Once they strayed a little from strict Puritan teachings to vote by a majority of one that reading, "fictitious writings" was more beneficial than injurious. On the day

---

47. *Ibid.*, 1, 63, 65, 67, 68, 146, 147.
48. Smyth, *Denominational Education*, 3.
49. Thalian Minutes, 8, 9, 35, 36, 41, 42, 68, 69.

after Fort Sumter was evacuated, they asked, "Ought public opinion be regarded as the Standard of right?" and answered *no* by a substantial majority. Shortly before, they had decided that representatives of the people ought to vote according to the dictates of their conscience and not be bound by the will of their constituents. Undoubtedly most Oglethorpe men opposed the use of strong drink, but in 1862 when many were fighting and dying for the Confederacy, the Thalians voted that war had done more harm than intemperance.[50]

The war spirit was reflected in the acts of the societies in other ways. As the conflict approached, the Thalians asked in May, 1860, "Has a State the right to secede from the Union?" Naturally they voted in favor of disunion by a large majority. Two months later, the Phi Deltas decided that Negro slavery was the chief cornerstone of Southern civilization and ought to be extended into Mexico and Central America. At the first meeting following Georgia's secession in January, 1861, the Thalians raised the question, "Has any Government or Union of States the right of coercing a seceding member?" Before the time set for the debate, a call meeting was held to "select another subject." Apparently the answer was so obvious that no one was willing to take the negative.[51]

After the fighting began, the Thalians directed their attention increasingly to the subject of war in general. When they were not discussing the Southern struggle for independence, they were often debating the American Revolution or some of the many conflicts of England or of France. To keep abreast of the times, they bought books on military subjects and subscribed to the *Southern Illustrated*, the best periodical portraying the Confederate leaders. They showed their patriotism by electing into honorary membership, prominent Confederate officers, the most noted of whom was General Alfred H. Colquitt, of Georgia.[52] As noted above, already, while the war clouds were gathering, the Phi Deltas, with seemingly prophetic vision, had elected John B.

---

50. *Ibid.*, 48, 50, 64, 65, 97, 99, 103, 105, 110, 111. See also Smyth, *Denominational Education.*
51. Thalian Minutes, 56, 58, 89, 90; Gordon, *Progress of Civil Liberty*, 17.
52. Thalian Minutes, *passim*, especially pp. 143, 144.

Gordon, then a young lawyer without fame and with no experience as a soldier, but soon to become the greatest of all the 120,000 that Georgia gave the Southern army.[53]

As the war dragged slowly on, members were called into Confederate service and after the Conscription Act of May, 1862, only boys not yet eighteen remained to debate the mighty problems of the day. They became despondent at the prospects of going away to fight as soon as they reached the draft age. Their pessimism is noticeable both in the subjects of their debates and in their votes on them. Immediately after the Conscription Act went into effect, the Thalians asked, "Is the Government of the Confederate States likely to be perpetual?" They answered *no* by a good majority. Later they queried, "Is war ever justifiable?" Again they said *no*. Finally, in the last recorded debate before the University was closed, they argued "Was the Death of Genl. Jackson more lamented than that of Albert S. Johnson [*sic*]?" They answered *yes*, indicating that they believed that the loss of "Old Stonewall" was a huge blow to the Confederate cause.[54]

There was a great host of other questions that disturbed the literarians. In fact, nothing that engaged the attention of thoughtful men seemed to escape their notice. The range is too varied and miscellaneous to be profitably classified further, but included: "Is capital punishment justifiable?" "Ought the press to be without legal restriction?" "Which has done the greater service to truth, philosophy or poetry?" "Is the art of speech more profitable than writing?" and "Ought the protective policy or free trade principles to prevail?"[55] While the Thalians asked and answered these and many other questions, the Phi Deltas considered: "Should our Legislature refuse a separate amount of public funds to the Catholics for educational purposes?"[56] "What is the only sure means of ultimate success?"[57] "What are the obligations of civiliza-

---

53. Gordon, *Progress of Civil Liberty*, 1. See also Isaac W. Avery, *The History of the State of Georgia, from 1850 to 1881* (New York, 1881), 323.
54. Thalian Minutes, 121, 123, 147, 148, 149.
55. *Ibid.*, 53, 61, 62, 78, 79, 87, 89, 125.
56. *Federal Union*, April 3, 1860. This was a joint debate, the Thalian taking the affirmative and the Phi Deltas the negative.
57. William Henry Stiles, *Study, the Only Sure Means of Ultimate Success* (Milledgeville, 1854).

tion to the arts and science?"[58] and "What are the claims of the English language upon the critical study of English and American scholars?"[59]

The regular Saturday meetings when usually these questions were disputed did not furnish enough time to fill the literarians' immense interest in debate and public speaking. There were special days when they could display their talent before the world in all their pomp and glory. For such occasions various members were chosen for the coveted honor of representing the society, and Thalians and Phi Deltas marched in processions to the chapel, with banners flying, and all wearing their emblems and other regalia. There they listened attentively to their orators and applauded their own men wholeheartedly. When the meeting was over, they returned to their halls and congratulated the winners.[60]

The first in the year of these public programs was the celebration of George Washington's birthday. In the early days of the republic Americans were more enthusiastic in honoring "the Father of his Country" and rarely failed to have appropriate exercises on February 22. On this day the societies took charge for the University. A joint committee arranged for music and invited all the military companies of Baldwin County and the public to attend the exercises in the chapel. The orator of the day alternated between Thalians and Phi Deltas and was chosen by a joint committee. If there was not enough celebration at the University the literarians could go to Milledgeville, where the day was observed with a parade by the Baldwin Blues, whose ardor for honoring Washington even the most inclement weather failed to dampen. On one occasion, at least, they marched through mud and slush "as though the Sun were shining brightly. It was a creditable turnout, albeit many of their plumes resembled a frizzly chicken after a heavy shower, and their pants were nearly ruined."[61]

58. Johnson, *Obligations of Civilization to the Arts and Science.*
59. Benjamin Morgan Palmer, *The Claims of the English Language* (Columbia, S. C., 1853).
60. Thalian Minutes, *passim.*
61. *Federal Union*, March 2, 1858. See also Thalian Minutes, *passim.*

The Annual Contest, usually held near the end of the winter term, furnished the Thalians and Phi Deltas an opportunity to compete publicly for literary honors in debate, declamation, and written composition. The exercises were held in the chapel and crowds attended not only from Midway, but also from Milledgeville. To assure good attendance, special trains were run to the college. The program began with a declamation contest in which each society was represented by one sophomore. Then two seniors, one a Thalian and one a Phi Delta, read essays. Next came the debate with a single representative from the societies on each side.[62]

The most important joint celebration of the year was that of national Independence Day. Even before the literary societies were founded, on the first glorious Fourth after Oglethorpe began operation, in 1838, Dr. Beman inaugurated observance of the birthday of the nation "in a manner altogether worthy of the occasion." The students, faculty, and townspeople assembled in the new chapel to hear the college president speak "appropriately and fervently." The Declaration of Independence was read; "a chaste and patriotic oration" was delivered; and the benediction was pronounced by Dr. Talmage. In the afternoon the ladies of Midway prepared "an excellent and abundant Dinner," in compliment to the faculty and students of the University, of which they were singularly proud. Between two and three hundred guests were served under a grove, "where social intercourse and good feeling, over pleasant lemonade, and good cold water prevailed through the evening."[63]

After the literary societies were organized, they took charge for the University in the early 1840's. The day began with the awakening thunder of cannon and the strains of music coming from Milledgeville. Hither the students and some faculty members repaired to witness a parade of the Metropolitan Greys, the Baldwin Blues, and the Governor's Horse Guard. After the usual "eloquent oration," the public meeting broke up and the military companies adjourned to a banquet, where toasts were drunk to Washington,

---

62. *Federal Union*, April 20, 1858; March 27, 1869; April 3, 1860. See also Thalian Minutes, *passim.*
63. *Southern Recorder*, July 10, 1838.

the other heroes of the Revolution, the living statesmen, and everyone else of importance. Sometimes a toast was drunk to Oglethorpe University. In 1839, Captain A. H. Kenan, of the Metropolitan Greys, gave this toast to the University: "While she trains
her scholars, may she foster soldiers also!"[64]

When the Milledgeville exercises were over, the students returned to the college to hear two speeches—one by a member of
each society. At the close of the day there was always a "PICNIC,"
or dinner, to which the public, especially the young ladies, were
invited.

Once the July celebration was marred by a tragedy. Le Roy
P. McCutcheon, a Thalian, was scheduled to read the Declaration of Independence, but, alas! a horrible fate overtook him on
June 26, 1850. As he and his fellow classmate, Preston B. Luce,
were on their way to breakfast, a sudden bolt of lightning struck
their umbrella and "shattered it to atoms," killing both of them
instantly. Dr. Talmage conducted their funeral in the chapel and
chose as the text of his sermon, "Once hath God spoken; yea
twice have I heard, that power belongeth unto God" (Psalms,
62:11). The two young men, both candidates for the ministry, were buried in a common grave in the college cemetery.[65]

Immediately after the tragedy a meeting of the student body was
called and resolutions on the death of the young men were drawn
and unanimously adopted:

> How Mysterious are the ways of Providence! and how uncer-
> tain is human life!
> Man is like the flower in the field. Today it springeth up,
> tomorrow is cut down. His life is as a shadow; in a moment it
> fleeth and continueth not. His days are swift as the lightning by
> which our young friends fell.
> Man has his appointed time upon earth; of days he knows noth-
> ing and vanishes as a sunbeam. The uncertainty of human life;
> the solemn truth that man's days are numbered; the vanity of
> all earthly hopes have been strikingly illustrated in the sudden
> death of our companions. Only a day or two ago they walked

---

64. *Ibid.*, July 9, 1839.
65. *Ibid.*, July 2, 1850.

among us, and mingled in our college circle; on their cheeks glowed the bright hue of health, while their eyes spoke of hearts filled with buoyant hopes. But alas! Death, with unerring aim, sped his blow and numbered them with the "pale nations of the dead." How sudden was their fall! how affecting was their fate! called away without a moment's warning. The sad tidings have filled our hearts with mournful sorrow.

We feel that their demise has left a void in our midst, for they were kind, beloved, affectionate, possessing all the valued qualities that flow from generous souls; and above all they feared God. Their room was a room of prayer; and their evening vespers were but echoes of their morning devotions.

Yet our sorrow is mingled with feelings of joys and hope, for where the good die,
'Night dews fall not more gently on the ground,
Nor weary worn out winds expire so soft.'

The following week the Fourth of July found both Thalians and Phi Deltas wearing mourning instead of enjoying the birthday of the nation in the usual manner.[66]

A literary work begun in January, 1855, by the senior class, though not carried on by the society organizations, but in reality done chiefly by the members, was the *Oglethorpe University Magazine*. The O. U. M., as the periodical was familiarly called, was published monthly during the college year and usually contained about thirty-two pages, octavo. Each volume comprised ten issues and cost one dollar, "payable invariably in advance." The articles were written chiefly by the seniors, but some were contributed by the professors and Trustees and even by friends of the University. The subjects, usually serious, included a wide variety of topics. Historical, scientific, and philosophical studies, poems, short stories of fiction, moral essays, an occasional book review, and discussions of current problems of the day filled the pages of the O. U. M. Representative titles were "Thomas Moore" (the first article in the first number), "Tullulah Falls" (a poem), "Capital Punishment" (by Professor Smith), "The Lover's Farewell, A Melting Scene," "Few Errors of College Life," "A Lesson from the Book of Nature," "A Glance at the Social and

---

66. *Federal Union*, July 2, 9, 1850.

Political Conditions of America," and "Kissing in France" (by E. A. Nisbet, chairman of the Board of Trustees). Not all that was submitted was accepted, and the reasons for rejection furnished material for editorial comment. One modest contributor who signed his name "Philomel" to two articles was warned that if he did not improve his penmanship, the editor would not accept any more of his literary efforts worthy though they might be.

To secure subscribers the editor advertised in the local newspapers before publication of the magazine began. Appeals were made to professors, alumni, and friends of the University; and students wrote to parents to secure their financial support. In the third issue ninety-five subscribers were named, and three months later the number was over a hundred. But at one dollar per person the hundred odd dollars from subscriptions was not enough to finance the O.U.M. and after seven issues it ceased publication.[67]

A major objective toward which both Thalians and Phi Deltas worked was building up their society libraries. Books were always acceptable and proper gifts, and each society secured many volumes from both honorary and regular members as well as from the faculty, and other friends of the University. In 1859 twelve friends gave the Thalians David Hume's *The History of England* and Edward Gibbon's *The History of the Decline and Fall of the Roman Empire*.[68] James H. Nichols presented the Phi Delta library *The Final Memorials of Charles Lamb* (edited by Thomas Noon Talfourd, New York, 1858). This work and Volumes III and IV of Hermann Ols-Lausen's *Biblical Commentary on the New Testament* (4 vols. translated by A. C. Kendreck, New York, 1857) are all that have survived from the Phi Deltas' collection of about two hundred and fifty books.[69] The Thalian library was larger and probably contained nearly a thousand volumes when the University was closed. Only four of them are still extant in Thalian Hall: Volume I of Robert Walsh's *Didactics: Social, Literary, and Political* (Philadelphia, 1836); Volume VI of *Posthumous*

---

67. The only complete file of the *Oglethorpe University Magazine* known to the present writer is in the George Barnsley Papers in the University of North Carolina Library.
68. Thalian Minutes, 3.
69. In the Sidney Lanier Room in Thalian Hall.

Works of the Rev. Thomas Chalmers, D.D., LL.D. (edited by William Hanna, New York, 1849); Volume I of *History of Spain and Portugal* (New York, 1840); and Volume I of *Greyslear, A Romance of the Mohawk* (n.p., n.d.).

The literary societies did not wait for others to make them gifts. As individual members, they bought and gave what they could afford, and each society liberally spent money for the purchase of books. On one occasion the treasurer of Thalia was ordered "to buy as many books as the state of the treasury will allow." Not even the War Between the States stopped the purchase of books. As late as March 6, 1863, a committee was sent to Macon to buy books.[70]

Gifts other than books were acceptable. In October, 1860, "A valuable Atlas was presented to the [Thalian] Society and received, and thanks were returned to the gentlemen" who gave it. Mrs. B. A. Sosby of Columbus gave some pictures for the new Thalian Hall just before the Society moved in. At the same time a map was received for the new building. Miss Laura Tucker sent the society "the tooth of a sea-reptile."[71]

Thalians and Phi Deltas soon forgot much that they learned in the classrooms at old Oglethorpe, but their training in literature and public speaking they carried with them to use until the end of their days. In the societies many became conscious for the first time of their latent ability or oratorical powers. Finding and developing those talents, they turned to the fields in which they could use them and became writers, college professors and presidents, public school teachers, doctors, lawyers, news editors, and a host of ministers of the Gospel, some of them the most noted in the Southern Presbyterian Church.

William J. Sasnett, a member of the first graduating class and a founder of Thalia, was the first of many Oglethorpe alumni who published a book—*Progress* (Nashville, 1855). He was a Methodist minister, a professor at Emory College, and president of La Grange (Georgia) Female College.[72] James Stacy, of the class of 1849, was active in the Thalian society and here displayed his budding

---

70. Thalian Minutes, 143.
71. *Ibid.*, 19, 73.
72. *Thalian Catalogue*, 1858, pp. 3, 10.

literary talent. He was the valedictorian of his class and spoke on "The Mission of Rome."[73] He became a Presbyterian minister and an authority on the history of his church.

Isaac W. Avery, a Phi Delta, won the sophomore declamation medal in 1852 and two years later showed his interest in current events when he spoke at commencement on "The Nebraska Bill."[74] After the War Between the States, he was an excellent orator, editor of the *Atlanta Constitution,* and author of *The History of the State of Georgia, 1850-1881,* the best source book on the period regardless of its faults.[75]

The Lanier brothers showed their first literary spark in the Thalian society. Clifford was an active member and developed his talent faster than Sidney. Though Clifford, as a writer, is usually considered inferior to his more famous brother, the former was able to find a publisher for his first book, but the poet had to hire one. For Sidney, Thalia was his most important contact at Oglethorpe. In reference to the society he wrote his father: "I have derived more benefit from that, than from any one of my collegiate studies. We meet together in a nice room, read compositions, declaim, and debate upon interesting subjects."[76] He joined the society during his first term in college, was a junior orator, senior essayist, president of Thalia, a regular debater and declaimer, and commencement speaker in 1860.[77] If the literary societies of Oglethorpe University had done nothing more than waken the genius of Sidney Lanier, that alone would have justified their existence.

73. *Southern Recorder,* Nov. 20, 1849.
74. *Ibid.,* July 21, 1852; July 23, 1854.
75. *The National Cyclopedia of American Biography* (35 vols., New York, 1891-   ), III, 828.
76. Mims, *Sidney Lanier,* 31-32.
77. Thalian Minutes, *passim.*

CHAPTER V

Religion and Science

PREACHING and praying consumed more time at Oglethorpe than debating, declaiming, and public speaking. The University had been founded primarily for the preparation of men for the Presbyterian ministry, and this object was persistently pursued throughout its history. Of course, most of the students who matriculated at Oglethorpe had no thought of becoming ministers, but the faculty through their own godly lives, fervent preaching, and continual praying hoped to convert the unsaved and to steer the saved into that profession.

To achieve these goals, the whole program of the University was directed, and the daily schedule was conformed. Students were required to arise at 6 A.M., and thirty minutes later everyone had to be in chapel for morning prayers. Then came breakfast at 7 o'clock, after which students went to their rooms to prepare their lessons, but some used this period for private devotion. At 8:30 classes began, when professors, regardless of the subject taught, found the Bible an ever-ready reference book. "The practical result was," estimated one student, "we received ¾ religion and ¼ worldly instruction."[1] At 5 P. M., when classes were finished, all returned to the chapel to hear some professor pray for forgiveness for the sins committed since sunrise and to warn the unsaved against the wrath to come.

On Tuesday nights the student body was refreshed by a walk to the Midway Church to listen to another exhortation from a visiting minister. On other evenings there were often special private

---

1. George Barnsley, "Recollections of Oglethorpe University," 6. In the summer months students were required to rise at 5 A. M. Barnsley to his father, June 16, 1855. In the Godfrey Barnsley Papers, Duke University Library.

prayer meetings held by the students in the dormitories or by faculty members in their homes. No one was required to attend, but there was a sort of taboo of any student who was regularly absent.

The religious program reached its climax on the weekends. As has already appeared, all of Saturdays was given to the literary societies. This was done not merely to train students in public speaking, but more especially to perfect the forensic talents of embryo preachers. That students' minds should not dwell on mundane things on the Sabbath all lesson assignments for Monday were made on either the English Bible or New Testament Greek or Evidences of Christianity.[2] On Sunday there were no morning prayers, but in order to afford plenty of time for a long sermon, services in the chapel began at 10 A.M. In the late afternoon at 5 o'clock there was a shorter sermon followed by a prayer meeting.

During the week faculty members preached daily at the chapel exercises. It was the special duty of the president of the University to lead these services, but he was often assisted by the professors. Dr. Talmage's messages were well received by the students. One of them thought he was "a cultured and refined gentleman, and a sincere undogmatic Christian. We all were pleased when he preached, for his words were ever seeking to excite us to endeavor, and was not covered with the dust of past theological thought. We listened as young men to the simple pure truth of Christian[it]y and were glad to go in the ways of peace and harmony."[3]

Dr. Smith's performance in the pulpit was not so gentle, but was far more impressive. "He was eloquent," recalled one Oglethorpe man, "and when he started preaching more or less according to Moses, there always seemed to appear a shimmering light as before a thunder storm. When that thunder rolled, the backsliders had to get under cover, and when he talked he brought into vision a vivid scene of hell-fire and torment that made us tremble who had done or were thinking of any fun. These ser-

2. Cf. *Oglethorpe University Catalogue*, 1857, p. 22.
3. Barnsley, "Recollections of Oglethorpe University," 3.

mons drove all the gaiety of youth from us, and we would return
to our rooms to moan in whispers of our misdeeds. He was an
orthodox Presbyterian and *knew* that he was right. He was a
commander of a ship, secure himself, and used every endeavor to
save the mariners of the sea of Life from a shipwreck on the ocean-
wastes of Eternity."[4]

So much religion produced amazing results in the lives of both
students and faculty. By far the great majority of the students
yielded to this pious atmosphere and came away from Oglethorpe
with Christian ideals and principles stamped firmly upon them,
if not professed Christians. As noted above, nearly a fourth of
the graduates entered the ministry or other religious work; at
least seven matriculates became preachers of the Word; and three
professors—Crawford, Lane, and Woodrow—who joined the faculty as laymen were caught up by the spiritual fervor at the University and were ordained.[5]

The Christian influence of the faculty spread far beyond the
University campus. Mention has already been made of Dr. Talmage's preaching at the Georgia Insane Asylum and at other
places throughout Georgia and even in neighboring states. His
example was generally followed by the other professors who
were ordained ministers. Dr. Lane regularly filled the pulpit at
Madison, Greensboro, and Milledgeville; and Dr. Smith preached
to congregations in Sparta, Eatonton, Monticello, Eastman, and
sometimes in the Independent Presbyterian Church in Savannah.[6]
After Dr. Woodrow entered the ministry in 1860, he often made
long excursions into the country to fill preaching appointments
on the weekends. He held services "in feeble churches and in
schoolhouses, court houses, and private houses, within forty or
more miles of the college; trying," he explained, "to make my
Sunday night services come within twenty-five miles of home,
so that I could drive to the college in time for my Monday morning sunrise lecture."[7]

4. *Ibid.*, 4.
5. See Appendix, *infra*, 165-168.
6. Allen, "Old Oglethorpe University," 56, 61.
7. Mims, *Sidney Lanier*, 30.

No member of the faculty sought more earnestly and unselfishly to spread the Gospel beyond the University campus than did Dr. Ferdinand Jacobs, professor of mathematics and astronomy, 1845-1849. Before coming to Oglethorpe, he was pastor of the Yorkville (South Carolina) Presbyterian Church, but his salary was so small that he had to teach in the local academy to make enough to support his family. After he came to Midway, he continued to preach for little or no salary, while he made his living teaching in the University. Once a month he filled the pulpit at Eatonton, twenty-four miles away, and three Sundays in the month he performed the thankless service of preaching to the prisoners in the State Penitentiary at Milledgeville. He often talked to the inmates of their sins and crimes, but usually they affirmed their innocence, or said that there were such palliating circumstances as to condone their actions. Though Dr. Jacobs felt that he accomplished little good because of the prisoners' unwillingness to repent, he continued to work among them until he was forced to resign from Oglethorpe in 1849 when the University could no longer pay his salary.[8]

Some of the students were so anxious to enter the ministry that they could not wait to finish the college course to begin working for the Master. In his sophomore year Groves Cartledge, of the class of '45, commenced the study of theology privately under Dr. Talmage. He applied himself so earnestly that his health was impaired, but before graduation he "went over the whole field of theological work, except Hebrew." While he was thus engaged, he accidentally formed a friendship with a rich planter, who was not a Christian. The planter was so impressed with Cartledge's sincerity that he assisted him financially and in time joined the church.[9]

John Elbert DuBose, of the class of '60, labored with untiring energy and zeal in Christian work while he was in college and later

---

8. Dr. Thornwell Jacobs, grandson of Dr. Ferdinand Jacobs, furnished this information. See also Thornwell Jacobs, ed., *William Plumer Jacobs, Literary and Biographical* (Oglethorpe University, Ga., 1942), 553-554.
9. Groves H. Cartledge, *Sermons and Discussions, with an Autobiography* (Richmond, Va., 1903), 24-28.

FERDINAND JACOBS

From a photograph in the possession of his grandson,
Thornwell Jacobs, who refounded Oglethorpe

CHARLES WALLACE HOWARD
*From a photograph loaned to the Georgia State Archives by
Mrs. Mary Howard Lebey, of Savannah*

at Columbia Theological Seminary. During his vacations he conducted religious services, organized Sunday schools, conducted Bible classes, and distributed religious books and tracts. "I fear," he once said, "I may not live to preach, and necessity is laid upon me to work while I live." When remonstrated by his classmates for imprudently exposing himself to inclement weather, he replied: "The night soon cometh when no man can work." Fearing that he might not live to preach, he endeavored to persuade every young man whom he met that it was his duty to preach the Gospel, unless he could give a good reason for not entering the ministry.[10]

George Whitfield Ladson, of the class of '59, was especially concerned with the religious instruction of the colored people. While preparing to enter Oglethorpe, he established a Sunday school for them in Roswell, Georgia, and was instrumental in having a church built for their use. He also gave the leisure he could afford from his studies to labors among the factory workers of the Roswell Manufacturing Company. After he enrolled at Oglethorpe, he began holding prayer meetings through the week for the Negroes in the vicinity and collected a large number of them into Sunday schools in the neighboring village of Scottsboro, conducting one school for children and one for adults. He was remarkably successful in the conversion of many of his colored pupils.[11]

George Scarbrough Barnsley, of the class of '57, who entered Oglethorpe to prepare for the Presbyterian ministry, had little success in converting his Episcopal family to the stern Puritanism he was studying in college. At the end of his sophomore year (1855), he visted his father's plantation, Barnsley Gardens,[12] near Cassville, and began his religious endeavors by preaching to the slaves and white workers, who listened to him respectfully. Some promised to sin no more, but soon they forgot and continued

10. *Memorial Volume of the Semi-Centennial of the Theological Seminary at Columbia, South Carolina* (Columbia, 1884), 263-264.
11. *Ibid.*, 306-307; Wilson, *Necrology*, 216.
12. Lucian Lamar Knight in *Georgia's Landmarks, Memorials and Legends* (2 vols., Atlanta, 1913-1914), I, 27-30, gives a colorful description of Barnsley Gardens.

their old way of living. Then young Barnsley argued with his sisters and his brother Lucian that their Episcopal creed was wrong and that they should live more puritanical lives. They laughed him to scorn, and Lucian would interrupt his brother's private sermons to describe the gay parties and balls that he had enjoyed in New Orleans during the previous winter.[13]

A few weeks before George had come home for the summer vacation, he read an article on "Novels" in the *Oglethorpe University Magazine*. The article warned:

"The influence which novels exert on the literary and moral tone of society is so great, that it becomes the duty of every true philanthropist to examine well whether this influence be likely to prove a blessing or a curse.

"Life is the time allotted to prepare the mind for eternity; and every work, that tends to divert the mind from the great object of its existence, is pernicious in the extreme.

"Now even if it were true that all novels were pure in language and sentiment, yet, when issued in such excessive numbers as they are *now*, they are productive of incalculable mischief. They have assumed by far the most prominent part of the literature of the day, and the minds of hoary headed age, and inexperienced youth, are alike abstracted from the solid truths of life, and made to wander in the illusory realms of fancy.

"Persons are often so completely spell-bound by reading novels, that they take no interest in studying anything else. The famished does not seize upon his prey with greater avidity than the novel reader upon the last new novel. Alas! after years spent in reading the most popular novelists, nothing really has been gained. . . .

"That novels are enemies to rational liberty and human progress is evident from the fact that they scatter the seeds of dissipation and vice, and tend to check all deep researches and noble aspirations after truth as it is contained in the pages of history, philosophy, and the Bible—the cornerstones of civilization. Where these are not studied, genuine freedom and real happiness are alike unknown.

---

13. Barnsley, "Recollections of Oglethorpe University," 15.

"War, famine, and the intoxicating bowl, are scarcely more grievous scourges than the novels, for the former have intervals of cessation, or are generally confined to the lower classes of society, but novels are ever present, and forever ensnaring the most promising youth, especially the fairest part of humanity.

" 'Tis said that a flower grows upon the banks of the Nile of a beautiful and enticing appearance, but that its leaves conceal the deadly asp, and if handled at all are liable to impart a sting of indescribable anguish and pain. So with novels. Pretending to be founded on facts the principles of virtue, they yet contain a poison more deadly than that of the asp, one that destroys the mind and the soul."[14]

George Barnsley was greatly impressed by the wisdom of these words and decided that he would give his sisters and brother a practical demonstration of the value of what he had learned at college, as they had laughed at his puritanical preaching. To illustrate his lesson, he collected from the library in the mansion some of the novels of Dickens, Thackeray, and Scott and made a bonfire of them. His action had the opposite effect to what he had anticipated. Everyone laughed and made fun of him. He later reported, "I became as rigid as a Scotch deacon, and was only consoled when the time arrived to go back to College." By that time George had lost much of his religious fervor and became more interested in science during his junior year.[15]

As George's interest in science increased, his enthusiasm for religion lessened. He soon took a special disgust for the old chapel bell that called students to prayers. He thought: "The sound of the bell was discord and it had a sharp cruel ring to it, which seemed to say, 'get up! get up! get up!'—Quickly—and then a long base note, 'come to prayers, you sinners.' There was not a vibration of pity or love or an echo of a soothing chord.—If we were sleeping and dreaming of homes and smoking or laughing in our dreams, we woke up suddenly to recollect Prof. Smith and backsliding."[16]

---

14. Tyro, pseud., "Novels," *Oglethorpe University Magazine*, I, 5 (May, 1855), 153-155.
15. Barnsley, "Recollections of Oglethorpe University," 7.
16. *Ibid.*, 7.

Another student developed an even greater dislike for the chapel bell and resolved to do something about it. In some way he gained admission to the belfry, which, it was whispered about as an open secret, was haunted. Climbing up the steep, narrow stairs, he tied a strong fishing line to the bell clapper and then passed the cord down a lightning rod until it reached a window sill, where he fastened a grooved wheel over which the line slid. Then he arranged the freedom of the cord to a pulley and conducted it to his room in the first dormitory. He waited to demonstrate his contraption until there was a beautiful moonlight night and the students were abed and all was still except for Professor Smith, who was on patrol. When the professor started home, the bell began to clang steadily.

To catch the culprit, the professor used a ruse; he slunk in the shadows into Central Hall and quietly climbed the belfry. Here he could be seen by the mischievous student, who ceased to toll the bell as soon as Dr. Smith ascended to the upper landing. The professor looked everywhere, but found nothing. Then he descended, but when he reached the ground, the bell began to ring again more violently than ever. He climbed up again, stepping softly, but by the time he had gained the top of the stairs the bell was silent. He made a second examination, but was unable to find the cause of the disturbance. He came down and strolled over the campus, expecting to catch some student up after time for "Lights out." Finally he saw a candle burning in the dormitory nearest Central Hall. He went to the door and knocked, but found his suspect busily studying his Greek. While the professor chided the student for keeping late hours, the boy kept swinging his leg to which was tied the fishing line, and the bell continued to clang in jerky, rhythmic response. When Dr. Smith left, there was a brief silence, but after he returned home, the ringing was renewed. It was the following morning before discovery of the line was made, but the offender received little punishment for his prank.[17]

Having escaped his just deserts for his misconduct, this inven-

---

17. *Ibid.*, 8.

tive young genius planned to show how little he regarded Dr. Smith's fervent preaching. He discovered that the divine wore a wig of beautiful brown hair, and he conceived a plot to remove it. From the gallery of the chapel he managed to pass a silk string through pulleys along the ceiling to a spot just over the pulpit, and to the end of the string he fastened a fishhook and a weight, which could be raised or lowered at will.

On the following Sunday night Dr. Smith preached one of his "hell-fire and brimstone" sermons while his antagonist seated himself in the balcony. In the midst of a burst of eloquence, with invisible electric sparks flying, slowly unseen, the fishhook descended, got a firm grip on the beautiful brown hair, and then ascended so softly that the preacher did not feel his loss. He was amazed as he looked out over the congregation, and instead of tearful features, he beheld a great display of handkerchiefs over mouths and sparkling, mirthful eyes. He passed his hand over his brow, and lo his head, which was as smooth as an ivory ball, told its own story. Dr. Smith did not believe in modern miracles, but he could not help following the eyes of the congregation to where the hair sailed slowly away towards the ceiling. He continued his sermon, and sinners and backsliders were warned of their unpardonable wickedness.

The example of Dr. Smith's harasser was soon followed by other rebellious students who did not like the University's stern discipline and excessive emphasis on religion. A committee decided to invite a noted preacher to fill the pulpit on the following Sunday. To draw a large crowd, an announcement was printed and freely circulated on Saturday. Sunday came clear and beautiful, and the people flocked to the college chapel. Some of the students stood in front to welcome the guests, but the doors to the chapel were closed and nobody could find the keys. The crowd pressed up the steps and into the vestibule before finally the doors were opened. When the pressure was relieved, there was a rush for seats without a cast of eyes to the pulpit. After all were seated, Dr. Talmage's old white mule, which the boys had made to climb the high steps to the vestibule and had led to the platform, rose up and began to bray as though he were welcoming the congregation. The mule wore a pair of leather-framed spectacles, through which peered his large rolling eyes, while his long ears flapped to and fro.

Dr. Talmage had a good sense of humor, but he failed to find any fun in this practical joke. Several students were expelled, and for several years thereafter there was peace and quiet on the Oglethorpe campus.[18]

A few conscientious students were sincerely troubled by the inconsistencies between orthodox Presbyterianism of that day and the liberal thought acquired from the study of Greek philosophy and literature. Dr. Smith was a fine classical scholar who loved the culture of the Hellenes almost as much as the teachings of the Bible. When he lectured on the Greeks, he usually spoke eloquently, but one day he burst forth, "like volcanic Etna, in peace and sunshine," in a vivid portrayal of the beauties of Hellenic sculpture, architecture, and intellectual achievements that inspired at least one of his students to delve deeper into classical thought.

Several days later, Dr. Smith spoke at one of the numerous prayer meetings on "The Proofs of the Divine Revelation of the Bible." With a large Bible spread open before him and with his long scrawny arms and hands extended over the Holy Writ, he rose to his six feet or more of height and proclaimed, "This is the Word of God; and anyone who has not read, and accepted this Book is doomed to everlasting punishment in Hell." He spoke like the captain of a ship that was about to be wrecked, and then lowering his voice, he added, "Possibly some of you do not quite comprehend me, and for such it will please me to have a call at my home."

George Barnsley listened to Dr. Smith with intense interest. After the prayer meeting the young man went to his room and reflected over the professor's arguments for the divine revelation of the Bible. George was in a dilemma. Dr. Smith had described the ancient Greeks as wonderfully intelligent and fine people. But how could they have accepted the Bible when they never heard of it and when much of it was not written until after

18. *Ibid.*, 9-10.

their day? To dissipate the fog of ideas, the student determined to pay Dr. Smith a visit and ask him to explain himself.

"Professor," he began, "you gave in our class some days since a most interesting and vivid description of Athens etc. I have read and studied books since and I am very much interested. In your lecture on the Bible the other day you declared that whoever never heard of or read this Bible went to Hell.—I came to ask you, according to your invitation, 'What has become of those great thinkers and splendid men of Greece?' "—Are they lost?' "

The professor looked at George as though he questioned the boy's sincerity. Then reading in his eyes that he was in dead earnest, he reflected a moment and answered, "It is to be supposed that God has made for them some other dispensation." George thanked Dr. Smith and went to his room, but he was not satisfied. He sorrowed for the Greeks and all those noble men of Rome such as Cicero and Plutarch.

George was so troubled that night that he could not sleep. He read the New Testament in Greek and meditated prayerfully over it. Finally he concluded that if the best men of ancient Athens and Rome were in Hell, surely the nether regions could not be such a bad place after all. Furthermore the descriptions of Heaven that he had heard at Oglethorpe were only of a place where you "flap your wings periodically and shout 'Hosannas,' which had no intellectual life in it; in Hades at least there would [be] stirring times." And then and there poor George decided that he was not one of God's elect, though he had tried to be. Thereafter he attended only those religious services required by the University, and turned to the study of geology and mathematics with renewed vigor.[19]

Calvinistic theology, as taught by most Oglethorpe professors, held that life on this earth was chiefly a period of struggle and hardships in preparation for the world to come. But Dr. Le Conte believed, "Life is a time of happiness as well as of struggle. Life is intended for enjoyment as well as for battle."[20] This view was shared by many Oglethorpe students, who were as anxious and

---

19. *Ibid.*, 16-18.
20. Joseph Le Conte, *Religion and Science* (New York, 1877), 45.

willing to enjoy their college days as are young people today.

After George Barnsley decided that he was not one of the elect, he gave up his determination to become a minister and began to seek a few worldly pleasures. A month later, during the spring holidays (April, 1856), he and W. H. Harris made a boat trip to Darien, Georgia, at the mouth of the Altamaha River. George had a plank skiff built in Milledgeville, and he rigged up a mast and sail out of a bed quilt. As soon as the "Little Commencement" exercises were over, the two boys set out with hired men to carry their baggage and sail to the Oconee River. After a very perilous voyage of about a week, they arrived at Darien. By that time a rumor had spread over the Oglethorpe campus that the vacationers were drowned. When they returned, classes had already begun, but the faculty was so glad to see them alive they were not called to account.

Having become a man of the world, George soon yielded to sin. He hired Steve, Dr. Smith's mulatto, to steal one of the professor's turkeys. George later related, "Steve did not make a good selection—it was lean and tough. I was late getting to breakfast next morning, and as my praying-associates met me going some one whistled, and they gobbled as turkey-cocks. I was a derelict, but did not go astray, only once when I danced at a stagg[*sic*]."[21]

No dancing was allowed on the campus, but on the night after commencement in 1857, some of the seniors gave a "Hop" at Brown's Hotel in Milledgeville. The dance was well attended and Governor Joseph E. Brown and Honorable Benjamin H. Hill were present. Supper was served "in the Brownest style" and prepared "with much taste and in great abundance." At 2 P.M. one special guest left "the young people still hopping, and very much disposed to hop all night, till the broad day-light, and go home with the gals in the morning."[22]

Some students who cared little for worldly pleasures were greatly puzzled by the apparent, if not real, conflict between religion and science. Professor Le Conte tried valiantly to answer this problem while he was professor of geology and natural science

21. Barnsley, "Recollections of Oglethorpe University," 24.
22. *Federal Union*, July 28, 1857.

in 1852. As early as 1845 he had read Robert Chambers's *Vestiges of a Natural History of Creation*, which was his first introduction to the theory of evolution.[23] The book interested Le Conte very much, but he rejected Chambers's thesis, not because he thought it conflicted with the Bible, but because "it was essentially a reproduction of Lamarck's views in a more popular form. It was not a truly scientific work nor written by a scientific man."[24]

Later, when Darwin published his *On the Origin of Species* in 1859, Le Conte read the work and reluctantly accepted the doctrines of natural selection and survival of the fittest. Within a few years, however, he became "an evolutionist, thorough and enthusiastic," accepting the hypothesis, as he explained, "not only because it is true, and all truth is the image of God in the human reason, but also because of all the laws of nature it is by far the most religious, that is, the most in accord with religious philosophic thought."[25]

While Le Conte taught at Oglethorpe, he did not believe and could not have believed in the Darwinian theory, for it was not published until seven years after the professor resigned to accept a position at the University of Georgia. But while he was at Oglethorpe, he began to observe the apparent irreligious and materialistic implications of science, and as a sincere Christian strove earnestly to show in his courses in geology and natural history the divine plan. In thus trying to reconcile religion and science, he did his students a great service, and at the same time he was preparing himself for the role he was to play in combating the materialistic and un-Christian implications of the theory of evolution.[26]

The good work begun by Dr. Le Conte was continued by Dr. Woodrow, who, one student thought, "had a sore time in teaching geology on account of Adam's biography" as recorded in Genesis.[27] The professor rested his attempt to harmonize scrip-

---

23. *Autobiography of Joseph Le Conte*, 105.
24. Joseph Le Conte, *Evolution and Its Relation to Religious Thought* (New York, 1888), 34.
25. *Autobiography of Joseph Le Conte*, 336.
26. *Ibid.*
27. Barnsley, "Recollections of Oglethorpe University," 4.

ture and science upon the thesis that "the God of nature and the God of revelation are one and the same." He argued: "Geology, in the opinion of wise men, instead of throwing discredit upon the Bible history of man and the world, is destined to become one of the ablest and most convincing supporters of the truth of that history. By means of it we are enabled to draw forth proofs of the authenticity of the divine record, even from the heart of the earth, sufficient to fasten conviction upon the infidel and atheist. . . .

"Turn our eyes, where we may, and the great volume of nature stands with open leaves inviting us to look and learn. Take any one of the branches of natural science, follow it out with careful study into its ramifications, and it will be found that no source of knowledge furnishes purer pleasure or more permanent benefit. The beautiful workmanship charms and delights us, while the evident design manifest in everything around us, clearly and forcibly leads our minds up to the contemplation of that Great Being who is the author of them all."[28]

Edward O. Frierson, one of Dr. Woodrow's students, wrote just before he was graduated in 1855 an essay on "The Existence of God Proved by the Light of Nature." He reasoned: "If we light upon a piece of mechanism though before unknown to us, and observe that it is adapted to secure definite ends, the conclusion is irresistible, that it is the result of contrivance, and that the contriver is an intelligent agent. If we apply this mode of reasoning to account for the existence of animate beings in nature, conviction is fastened on the mind that each individual creature is the result of a distinct purpose in the mind of an intelligent Creator. Thus we find every creature endowed with instincts and physical conformation of parts adapted to secure its sustenance and comfort in the position in which it enters upon existence."[29]

Professor Woodrow's success in teaching his students science

---

28. Philomel, *pseud.*, "Geology and the Bible," *Oglethorpe University Magazine*, I, 4 (April, 1855), 108, 111, 112. If Philomel was not Dr. Woodrow, he was certainly one of his students, reflecting the professor's thoughts.
29. Julius, *pseud.*, "The Existence of God Proved by the Light of Nature," *Oglethorpe University Magazine*, I, 4 (April, 1855), 9-10. Julius is identified as E. O. Frierson by George Barnsley. See Barnsley Papers in the University of North Carolina Library.

so as not only not to contradict his Bible but also to support the Holy Word attracted the attention of Southern Presbyterians. During the late fifties the synods of Georgia, South Carolina, Alabama, and Mississippi were becoming increasingly disturbed by "the inroads of infidel scientists on Christianity." When Darwin's *On the Origin of Species* was published, the synods first passed urgent recommendations and vehement resolutions. Then the Reverend James A. Lyon, a vigorous pastor in Mississippi, persuaded Judge Perkins, a member of his church and a planter who lived at "The Oaks" near Columbus, to endow a theological chair "to evince the harmony of science with the records of our faith, and to refute the objections of infidel naturalists." The Synod of South Carolina thereupon established at Columbia Theological Seminary "the Perkins Professorship of Natural Science in Connection with Revelation," the first such chair ever created. For this position the Synod of Georgia decided to elect Dr. Woodrow.[30]

When Woodrow assumed the new professorship in January, 1861, there were some who feared in the election of the Heidelberg graduate an emphasis on science rather than on theology. Others hoped that he would succeed in embarrassing, perhaps even confounding, "infidel science." But Dr. Woodrow at the outset shifted from "harmony of Scripture and science" to "lack of contradiction" between the two.[31] His fundamental thesis was: "The Bible and nature are both from God. They cannot be contradictory. Apparent conflicts arise from misinterpretations of one, or the other, or of both. Remove these conflicts by ascertaining and interpreting correctly the facts of both."[32]

For the next quarter of a century he developed and impressed these principles upon successive classes in the Theological Seminary, just as he had done at Oglethorpe. During this time he rose rapidly to a position of distinction in the Southern Presbyterian Church, and in 1884 he became a figure of nation-wide interest

30. P. E. Graham, "James Woodrow, Calvinist and Evolutionist," *loc. cit.*, 308-309; Woodrow, ed., *Dr. James Woodrow*, 13, 56-57.
31. Graham, *loc. cit.*, 309.
32. Woodrow, ed., *Dr. James Woodrow*, 15.

when he published his address on *Evolution,* delivered before the Directors of the Perkins Chair and the Alumni Association of the Seminary. The publication of the address led to his spectacular trial for heresy, which has already been discussed.[33] In 1888 the General Assembly condemned him as a heretic, though he persistently avowed his faith in the Bible and the Presbyterian creed, but his fight for the cause of truth was as great a victory as was that of Galileo with whom he was often compared. A recent writer has made the following evaluation of Woodrow's contribution to the progress of freedom of conscience both in religion and science:

Woodrow's lasting influence and his true significance come from his combining within himself a spiritual religion and modern science,—in his case, Calvinism and evolution. With a spiritual life dominated by one of the strictest of creeds and a respect for the truths of science amounting almost to reverence, he yet united these apparently far-separated realms of spirit and sense. Just as he was insisting upon retaining his spiritual beliefs (and incidentally, his church affiliation) without any limiting of his conceptions of science, he was also demanding the privilege of accepting physical truths, whatever their nature, without prejudice to his spiritual realities. And he was successful![34]

33. In the *Southern Presbyterian Review,* July, 1884.
34. Graham, *loc. cit.,* 315.

CHAPTER VI

The Light of Commencement

OGLETHORPE University opened its halls of learning in January, 1838, and soon its intellectual light began to shine in Georgia, the South, and the nation. At first the rays were so dim that they could scarcely be seen beyond Midway and Milledgeville, and few people outside of Baldwin County observed the glow of Oglethorpe's cultural brightness. The local weeklies, the *Federal Union* and the *Southern Recorder*, sometimes reflected the University's light in their columns with notices of special programs and other activities of the students and faculty. At the end of the first school year, in October, 1838, these newspapers reminded "the friends, patrons, and public at large" of Oglethorpe's closing exercises and invited every one interested to attend.[1] Though there were no graduates, the junior and sophomore oratorical contests showed Georgians that higher education was becoming refulgent in their state capital and that it was "a thing of beauty." Those who attended liked it and began looking forward to the time when Oglethorpe would have a graduating class.[2]

A year passed, and the University proudly celebrated its first commencement in the fall of 1839. The college was now two years old, and the time had come to show what its light of knowledge was doing for the youth of Georgia and the South. The Trustees and faculty agreed that every effort must be made to advertise the school through its finished products. As early as September 3, the *Southern Recorder* carried an announcement of the exercises that were to be held on October 31. To assure large attendance, it was repeated in each succeeding issue of the weekly throughout September and October, and the Columbus

1. *Southern Recorder*, Oct. 9, 30, 1838.
2. *Ibid.*

Enquirer, the Macon *Messenger*, the Augusta *Chronicle*, and the Savannah papers were asked to copy "twice" the notice of Oglethorpe's commencement.[3]

The exercises began at 10 o'clock Tuesday morning, October 29, with the Junior Exhibition, which was from beginning to end an oratorical fiesta. Each junior delivered an original address. In addition to the student speeches, which one hearer thought were marked by "sobriety and vigor of thought," there was a baccalaureate sermon by President Beman.[4] In the evening the annual meeting of the Board of Trustees was held.[5]

The next morning the four graduating seniors reigned supreme. Like the juniors, each graduate delivered an original address. These orations, reported one visitor, "were discussed with a manliness which gave substantial evidence of ability and usefulness in the future man of the world and a good evidence of the happy system of instruction pursued by this institution."[6] The degree of Bachelor of Arts was conferred on John H. Fitten, Thomas E. Loyd, and William J. Sasnett.[7] John B. Whitehead "was granted a testimonial of having creditably completed the *irregular course* of study." Sasnett became the first of Oglethorpe's long line of ministers.[8]

A special feature of this commencement season was the public examination of the senior class held a few days before graduation. The examining committee included the Reverend Thomas Goulding, later president of the Presbyterian Theological Seminary at Columbia, South Carolina; Joseph Henry Lumpkin, soon to be Georgia's first chief justice of its new supreme court; Charles J. Jenkins, a future governor of the state; and Absalom Harris Chappel, author of *Miscellanies of Georgia*. Before this distinguished Board of Examiners the seniors acquitted themselves well and won the approval of the listening public. "The examinations were thorough," related an observer, "and afforded the most satisfac-

---

3. *Ibid.*, *Sept.* 3, 10, 17, 24; Oct. 1, 8, 15, 22, 29, 1839.
4. *Ibid.*, Oct. 29; Nov. 5, 1839.
5. T. Minutes, 1835-70, *passim*.
6. *Southern Recorder*, Nov. 5, 1839.
7. T. Minutes, 1835-1872, p. 49.
8. *Ibid.*; Stacy, *Presbyterian Church in Georgia*, 151.

tory proof that at no institution, north or south, are young men better instructed than at Oglethorpe University."[9]

Thus the first commencement had proved a great success,[10] and henceforth until the University was closed during the War Between the States, the graduating season was attended by ever increasing throngs and was celebrated with the enthusiasm and pomp of a modern home-coming weekend when an intersectional football game is played. In 1840 Dr. Beman preached a baccalaureate sermon on Sunday preceding graduation day and thus lengthened the commencement to four days.[11] After Dr. Talmage became president in 1841, he continued this practice, and his baccalaureate addresses always attracted attention from far and wide. In 1849 the *Southern Recorder* commented: "The Commencement Sermons of Dr. TALMAGE have been all of so high and emphatically useful a character, that the country requires them to be furnished in a more enduring form and for a wider sphere of influence. We trust they may be collected by the Board of Trustees and given to the public at least at no distant day."[12]

Every conceivable means was used to draw large crowds to commencement. Citizens of Baldwin County were urged to "extend to strangers present those friendly courtesies that will render their visit to our place agreeable."[13] Private homes were opened to guests who came from all over the state and even from adjoining states. Occasionally a stranger came from afar, as in 1848 when the Reverend Thomas Houston, from Knockbreckan, Ireland, professor of theology in the Reformed Presbyterian Church, was present and two years later the Reverend John Stoughton, of London, England, attended.[14] In 1853 the new Midway Hotel was temporarily opened for the accommodation of visitors to commencement,[15] and the state legislature, if in session, sometimes adjourned to help swell the attendance.[16] Governor Herschel V.

---

9. *Southern Recorder*, Nov. 5, 1839.
10. *Ibid.*, Nov. 5, 1839.
11. *Ibid.*, Oct. 20, 27, 1840.
12. *Ibid.*, Nov. 13, 1849.
13. *Ibid.*, July 17, 1855.
14. *Ibid.*, Nov. 21, 1848.
15. *Ibid.*, July 12, 1853.
16. *Ibid.*, *passim*.

Johnson, who lived at Midway, often honored the graduating exercises with his presence.[17]

From the first commencement to the last the practice of inviting prominent speakers as a drawing card was employed. In 1840 Eugenius Aristides Nisbet, one of Georgia's leading lawyers and politicians, addressed the second graduating class before a "most imposing" audience.[18] Two years later the noted historian, William Bacon Stevens, spoke on "The Early History of Georgia."[19] In 1847 William Gilmore Simms addressed the literary societies on "Self-Development."[20] In 1855 Dr. James H. Thornwell, president of the University of South Carolina, spoke on "The Personality of God."[21] The next year Governor Johnson spoke on the "Obligations of Civilization to the Arts and Science."[22]

Other methods were used to boost the attendance. After the completion of the Milledgeville and Gordon Railroad, which ran through the college campus, special trains were run to Oglethorpe from Milledgeville during commencement week. Excursion trains from Eatonton, Gordon, and Macon brought passengers directly to the college. Even on commencement Sunday, trains were run from Milledgeville so the religious-minded could hear Dr. Talmage's baccalaureate address. The fare on all of these extra trains was half-price.[23]

In 1853 commencement season was moved back to the third week in July, where it remained until the War Between the States began. The summer weather helped swell the attendance so greatly that henceforth there were overflow crowds from Sunday through Wednesday. One who was present in 1860 reported that at every exercise the chapel was filled and on graduation day many could

17. *Ibid.*, July 29, 1856.
18. *Ibid.*, Nov. 10, 1840.
19. *Ibid.*, Nov. 22, 1842.
20. *Ibid.*, Nov. 9, Nov. 23, 1847.
21. *Ibid.*, July 24, 1855.
22. *Ibid.*, July 29, 1856. Copies of this oration can be found in the De Renne collection at the University of Georgia Library and in the pamphlet collection of the Duke University Library.
23. *Southern Recorder*, July 12, 1853; July 11, 1854; July 10, 1855; July 22, 1856.

not get seats downstairs in the main auditorium or in the balcony.[24] The dimensions of the chapel were forty-eight by sixty feet on the main floor and forty-eight by eleven in the balcony, making a total of 3,408 square feet. This space will easily seat over five hundred people.[25]

As the University grew older, commencement exercises increased in length. In 1848 the sophomore declamation contest was added to the already long list of attractions. Each literary society elected an equal number to compete and two prizes were given to the winners. On Monday evening, preceding graduation, the sophomores delivered memorized declamations though occasionally an ambitious student gave an original oration.[26] Usually the subject of the speech was patriotic or dealt with a current problem, such as "Slavery," "The Importance of Preserving the Union," "Responsibility of American Youth";[27] but literary and historical topics were quite common. In 1851 four sophomores declaimed on "Byron," "Cassius Instigating Brutus Against Caesar," "La Fayette," and "Field of Waterloo." One contestant composed his own speech on "Verginaud to the National Convention."[28] Up to the beginning of the War Between the States the declaimers seemed to have a strong preference for Whig and Union sentiment. If the titles of their speeches are a trustworthy index, Henry Clay and Daniel Webster were their favorite heroes. At first the number of speakers was small, but by 1859 there were twenty-two. To relieve the audience from the boredom of so much declaiming, each pair of speeches was punctuated by music.[29]

The sophomores were followed on Tuesday morning by the junior orators. They were expected to deliver original addresses, though occasionally they too gave declamations. In general the range of subjects varied little from those chosen by the second-year men—"The Destiny of our Country,"[30] "Henry Clay,"[31]

24. *Ibid.*, July 24, 1860.
25. Richards, ed., *Georgia Illustrated.* 7.
26. *Southern Recorder*, Oct. 24; Nov. 7, 1848.
27. *Ibid.*, Nov. 18, 1851; *Federal Union*, July 26, 1859.
28. *Southern Recorder*, Nov. 18, 1851.
29. *Federal Union*, July 26, 1859.
30. *Ibid.*, Nov. 18, 1851.
31. *Ibid.*, Nov. 16, 1852.

"Intellectual and Moral Culture," "British Tourists in America," and "Claims of Society upon the Educated."[32] Because there were fewer juniors than sophomores, the oratorical contests consumed a little less time than the delivery of the declamations, but the awarding of sophomore prizes and the address by the judge made the two programs of almost equal length. A prize was given to the best junior orator.

The sophomore and junior speeches always elicited comment from the press. Usually its remarks were commendatory, if not so laudatory as to seem flattery, but sometimes a speaker provoked harsh criticism, as did Sidney Lanier in his junior oration on "The Press." "When he gets a little older," wrote a newspaper editor, "he will find that *great* Reformations, such as he proposed, are not accomplished in a day or a year; and that they do not often receive their first impulse from the virgin efforts of College boys."[33] The length of the program more often than the subject matter of the orations called forth editorial comment. In 1848 when fourteen juniors spoke, the *Southern Recorder* suggested: "We have but a single remark to make; that respects the *length* of the speeches. The flesh is weak—too much of a good thing will clog the appetite."[34]

Wednesday was "the great day," as one person expressed it.[35] Shortly after sunup the crowd began to gather in the University chapel, and long before the graduating exercises began it was filled to overflowing. One who attended in 1858 described commencement day in this language: "The sun shone, the dusk crept lazily and heavily up—vehicles of every description rattled furiously along; beauty spread herself and shirt collars caved; fuss and feathers—cravats and crinoline—were the order of the Day. The Chapel groaned under the affliction of this heavy responsibility. Never have we seen a larger or more brilliant assemblage of modest maids and gallant gentlemen, gathered under the wings of our Fair Mother."[36]

32. *Southern Recorder*, July 27, 1858.
33. *Federal Union*, July 27, 1858.
34. *Southern Recorder*, Nov. 21, 1848.
35. *Ibid.*, July 24, 1860.
36. *Federal Union*, July 27, 1858.

In the early years of Oglethorpe each graduating senior was required to make a speech of original composition unless excused by the faculty.[37] By 1852 there were so many graduates that the number of speakers was cut to eight. The program began at 10 o'clock "sharp" with the delivery of the salutatory, often in Latin or Greek. Occasionally there were two salutatorians.[38] The subjects of the speeches were usually serious—"The American Scholar," "Defence of the Classics," "Progressive Spirit of the XIX Century,"[39] "The Value of Knowledge," "The Present Age,"[40] "Utilitarian Philosophy," and "The Progress of Man."[41] Rarely did a humorous title appear on the program as in 1844 when James R. Tucker spoke on *"Pastillos Rufillus olet;* or a Dissertation on Dandies."[42] The religious atmosphere that pervaded Oglethorpe was more generally observed in the addresses of the graduates. One person wrote: "Their speeches were distinguished for the moral and religious tone which pervaded them, which speaks highly for the faculty, in the religious influences with which they have surrounded their Institution."[43] Of course, the last senior speech was the valedictory, but because the faculty found difficulty in deciding who the best student was, there were sometimes two farewell addresses. The program of commencement in 1843 is reproduced below:[44]

Prayer by the President	
D. H. B. Troup, Darien, Ga.	*The American Constitution*
J. H. Nisbet, Midway, Ga.	*Astronomy, Excused*
A. H. Bowen, Clinton, Ga.	*Scotland*
J. N. King, Macon, Ga.	*Association of Ideas*
J. A. Hall, Midway, Ga.	*Influence of the Press on the Present Age*
R. A. Smith, Macon, Ga.	*The Statesman*

---

37. In 1851 four out of a class of eleven were excused. *Southern Recorder,* Nov. 18, 1851.
38. This was the case in 1853. *Federal Union,* July 26, 1853.
39. *Ibid.*
40. *Southern Recorder,* Nov. 20, 1849.
41. *Ibid.,* Nov. 19, 1844.
42. *Ibid.*
43. *Ibid.,* Nov. 16, 1852.
44. *Ibid.,* Nov. 21, 1843.

J. I. Neely, Washington Co., Ga.	*2nd Honor*
	The Fine Arts
G. S. Owens, Savannah, Ga.	*1st Honor*
	Life Pilgrimage
W. L. Franks,	*1st Honor*
	Valedictory
	Judicature of Georgia
Henry R. Jackson, Esq.	Anniversary Oration before the
	Thalian and Phi Delta Societies

At first, when there were few students, the program was relatively short, but as they increased in numbers, the length of the exercises increased correspondingly. Besides the senior speakers there was generally an address to the graduating class by a distinguished Southern orator. Alexander H. Stephens, Joseph R. Wilson, and William H. Crawford, Jr., were among those who thus performed at various times. At the close of the program, there was a recess after which the audience reassembled to hear an oration delivered before the two literary societies. This usually consumed another hour or more. (From the first commencement music was used to enliven the program.) The exercises were eventually concluded in the latter part of the afternoon.[45]

The lengthy programs aroused many complaints. A newspaper correspondent who attended commencement in 1858 said: "After the delivery of a dozen speeches from the graduating class, the conferring of Degrees, and the Address to the Sophomore Class, on the distribution of Prizes, human nature will not rest under another address of two hours length." This critic estimated that the exercises were fully of five hours duration. He hoped that at the next graduation they would be shortened to a mere two hours and a half.[46]

It would have stretched mortal patience beyond human endurance had good order been maintained throughout such long proceedings. A visitor in 1859 complained of "the intolerable noise in the galleries made by little boys, and the eternal clatter below, of silly girls and boys who seem to think that there is no-

---

45. *Ibid.*, Oct. 16, 1849.
46. *Federal Union*, July 27, 1858.

body present but themselves, or that all the company are as little interested as they are." He suggested as a remedy for this evil that Dr. Talmage thereafter appoint a police for the galleries and "point his finger at such parties below, as disturb the exercises by improper talking and laughing."[47]

A news editor at the same exercises wrote: "While our Commencements excel in their literary performances most other Colleges within our range of observation, we must say that they *excel all others in noise. . . .*"[48] At times conversation was carried on so loudly that it was impossible to hear the speakers. To secure better order, one friendly observer admonished commencement orators: "Give your visitors more wit, fun, spice and life in your selections and original pieces than are generally given. We do not expect, desire, or want learned disquisitions upon politics, religion, morals or science. Give your hearers something racy; for more talent and originality can be displayed in that way and more character made for smartness than many are apt to think. You can then claim the strict attention of your audience, and have less noise and talking."[49]

This same observer had a word regarding the strange custom of the ladies' throwing flowers on the stage after a favorite speaker had finished his oration. "The thing is carried to a ridiculous extreme," he said. "If the dear girls must throw boquets [*sic*], do not throw more than one or two to a speaker. It has ceased to be looked upon as a compliment or reward for merit, but thrown through mere partiality."[50] Another critic thought, "It is highly unbecoming in grown up people to engage in such practices."[51]

But the ladies' conduct was not entirely reprehensible. Without them commencement would hardly have been a success. They added the one thing that all college men most desired—feminine beauty. Of the ladies present on graduation day in 1844, it was said: "Beauty is never so radiant, as when it gilds the rugged path to the temple of knowledge, and cheers the gloom which often

47. *Ibid.*, July 26, 1859.
48. *Southern Recorder*, July 23, 1859.
49. *Ibid.*, July 24, 1860.
50. *Ibid.*
51. *Federal Union*, July 24, 1860.

envelopes the youthful and anxious devotee of truth."[52] For furnishing so much to the season's happiness, Southern chivalry demanded that the ladies be recompensed: There must be "sumptuous and tasteful entertainment," parties and dinners in their honor.[53] After attending the social gaieties of 1855, one person related, "It was pleasant and agreeable, and, judging from the joyous and cheerful faces of the young people," he knew "that all was well with them." Naively he added, "The supper was elegant."[54]

Sometimes the girls from Wesleyan College at Macon made their debut at Oglethorpe commencement "where they were pleasantly regaled by the budding eloquence and courtly chivalry of Georgia's future orators, statesmen and kings of the highway," related a graduate of the women's school. She long remembered: "We were splendidly entertained at the grand old colonial home of General and Mrs. Myrick, in Midway, a suburb of Milledgeville, which was near the University, and no one ever had a merrier time than those same Wesleyan girls, for there were carriages and dashing horses at their disposal, brave, gallant young hearts at every turn; brilliant parties in Milledgeville, and all that one could desire after climbing for months over trigonometrical problems and the uncongenial atmosphere of Cicero['s] De Senectute."[55]

In 1859 a special feature of commencement was the unveiling of a portrait of the aging president, Dr. Talmage. Some months before, the students, observing the failing health of their president, persuaded him to let them bear the expense of having his portrait painted. It was presented to the Board of Trustees by Stinson Little, a member of the graduating class. John T. Gresham, president of the Board, accepted it for the University. Dr. Talmage was noticeably moved by this token of appreciation on the part of the students.[56]

---

52. *Southern Recorder*, Nov. 19, 1844.
53. *Ibid.*, July 24, 1855.
54. *Ibid.*
55. An unidentified newsclipping in the Oglethorpe University Scrapbook of Ivan Allen, Sr., of Atlanta.
56. Jacobs, *The Oglethorpe Story*, 96-97.

An interesting part of the graduating exercises was the custom of conferring second degrees. These were not honorary, but rewards which could be claimed in the course of time. At first any person who held an A.B. degree from Oglethorpe, who was an alumnus of two years standing, and who attended commencement could receive a Master of Arts degree simply by applying for it. In 1852 the requirements for a second degree were raised. Thereafter the M.A. was not conferred upon candidates until three years after they earned the first degree, and they must prove they were "of good moral character" and were "engaged in some industrial or professional pursuit."[57]

The practice of conferring honorary degrees was common among colleges and universities of that day and was another means of attracting more people to commencement and at the same time enlisting the support of the alumni without which the modern institutions of higher learning could hardly survive. Oglethorpe began the custom in 1841 when John H. Fitten and William J. Sasnett, members of the first graduating class, were present to claim their M.A. degrees. Henceforth alumni came almost every year to receive this honor with all the rights and privileges thereunto appertaining.[58]

This manner of rewarding the alumni was paralleled by the granting of degrees to friends, patrons, and others who had or could in some way bring credit to the University. Oglethorpe began at the fourth commencement, in 1842, by conferring Masters of Arts on Alexander A. Smets, a prominent citizen of Savannah, and on Randolph H. Ramsay, principal of the Midway Academy for Boys. The University had been chartered ten years before it granted its first Doctor of Divinity degree. This honor was used rather sparingly and usually went to a deserving person, though of course to someone (usually a Presbyterian minister of distinction) who could advertise the school. In 1847 the Reverend Richard B. Cater was the first one upon whom this degree was conferred. After that, some years none was awarded, though in 1852 three were given. When the Reverend Thomas

---

57. T. Minutes, 1835-70, p. 147.
58. *Ibid.*, p. 73 and *passim*.

Houston traveled all the way from Knockbreckan, Ireland, to Midway in 1848, and the Reverend John Stoughton came from London two years later, they were made Doctors of Divinity. (Why not advertise Oglethorpe in Europe?) In 1853 the Reverend Carlisle P. Beman, first president of Oglethorpe and principal of Mt. Zion Academy, (which furnished the University many students) was likewise rewarded. In 1855 the Reverend James H. Thornwell, D.D., founder of the *Southern Presbyterian Review*, was given a Doctor of Laws. Three years later Joseph R. Wilson, pastor of the First Presbyterian Church in Augusta and father of Woodrow Wilson, was given the same degree.[59]

Two years before, Dr. Wilson had brought his family to the exercises and visited his brother-in-law, Dr. James Woodrow. The young professor was proud of Tommie, his young nephew, as Woodrow Wilson was then called. Looking admiringly at the child, as he sat on the floor playing with his rattle, Dr. Woodrow said to a student, "Did you ever see such a splendid dignified baby as Tommie? He looks to me like a moderator of a General Assembly." Over fifty years later, the student wrote, "Had he been a prophet he would have said President of the United States."[60]

There were others, unknown then, but destined to fame, who attended Oglethorpe commencements. On July 18, 1860, John B. Gordon was present to address the literary societies.[61] After Sidney Lanier, also destined to fame, had delivered his valedictory on "The Philosophy of History," Gordon spoke on the "Progress of Civil Liberty."[62]

He warned his audience: "The spirit of RESISTANCE is the spirit of LIBERTY; and He who holds in His own hands the destinies of nations, and is the Friend and Protector of constitutional liberty everywhere, is also the Friend and Protector of the institutions of the South; for, to-day African slavery is the

59. *Ibid., passim.*
60. Jacobs, *The Oglethorpe Story*, 98-99 n.
61. *Federal Union*, July 24, 1860.
62. Milton H. Northrup, "Sidney Lanier," *Lippincott's Magazine*, LXXV (March, 1905), 303; Clifford Lanier, "Reminiscences of Sidney Lanier," *Chautauquan*, XXI (July, 1895), 406.

SIDNEY LANIER

From an ambrotype in the possession of the family

JOHN B. GORDON, ESQ.

From a photograph in the National Archives, Washington, D. C.

Mightiest Engine in the universe for the civilization, elevation and refinement of mankind—the surest guarantee of the continuance of liberty among ourselves. Then let us do our duty, protect our liberties and leave the consequences with God, who alone can control them. Do this, and we shall secure to OURSELVES, at least, the principles of our great constitution, and the blessings consequent on the maintenance of those principles. Do this and the day is not far distant when the Southern Flag shall be omnipotent from the Gulf of Panama to the coast of Delaware; when Cuba shall be ours; when the western breeze shall kiss our flag, as it floats in triumph from the gilded turrets of Mexico's capital; when the well clad, well fed, Southern, christian slave shall beat his Tamborine and Banjo, amid the orange-bowered groves of Central America; and when a pro-slavery Legislature shall meet in council in the Halls of the Montezumas. And our foreign population, too, shall be encouraged by a successful resistance, on our part, to the aggressions of these Northern aggressors."[63]

It appears from the comments on his speech in the local papers that Gordon made a favorable impression on his distinguished audience. The *Federal Union* succinctly observed:

> The Oration before the Literary Societies by John B. Gordon, Esq., was indeed a treat. He is an orator by nature, and a cultivated and forcible writer. His address which we have not time to notice particularly, was listened to with marked attention and was most enthusiastically applauded.[64]

The *Southern Recorder* elaborated more fully:

> Mr. Gordon is a handsome speaker, and his subject was well written and well delivered. The closing partook of rather a political complexion, and was Southern Rights all over. Mr. Gordon was for protection to our slave property in its broadest sense, and was for expansion and extension. He wanted to see Cuba, Mexico, Central America, and even South America ours; and he wanted to see the "peculiar institution" carried into those countries. We thought that while his hand was in for keeping all that we have got, and getting all we can, he should have included

---

33. Gordon, *Progress of Civil Liberty*, 14-15.
34. *Federal Union*, July 24, 1860.

Africa also. He was, in our opinion, an unadulterated "fillibuster." We would advise our friend Gordon, however, to narrow his ideas and feelings to the present generation, for we can assure him that "our posterity" can take care of itself without any assistance from us, nor will they thank us for being so solicitous about them. Doubtless they, like ourselves, will like to have a little spice of life in acquiring Territory, therefore we should not deprive them of that pleasure. A distinguished friend in commenting upon it, said that it commenced with an eulogy upon liberty, but wound up with an eulogy upon slavery. But, upon the whole, we liked the speech.[65]

Doubtless most of the audience also liked Gordon's speech. Before another commencement season, many who had applauded were in Virginia fighting for "the peculiar institution" in behalf of which he had spoken.

---

65. *Southern Recorder*, July 24, 1860.

CHAPTER VII

War's Tragic Years

O N October 2, 1860, Oglethorpe University began the fall
term with as large an enrollment as that of the year before and
under as apparently bright prospects as at any time in its history.[1]
But only outwardly was there peace. The calm that had enveloped
the dreamy little village of Midway, where "young eyes looked
love and young lips sang soft songs to the music of the flute,"[2]
was gone. All during the fall, students, professors and townspeople thought and talked of the Presidential contest that was to
be settled on November 5. Members of the Thalian Society debated, "Do the signs of the times justify us in the belief that our
Republic will meet with the same fate of Greece and Rome?"[3]

As soon as it was learned that Abraham Lincoln, a "Black Republican" and a purely sectional figure, had been chosen President, even those most hopeful of peace feared secession and consequent war. On the day after the election one Oglethorpe freshman wrote to his mother: "I hear of nothing but disunion and
see only blue cockades fluttering in the wind. My politics are
practicable and honorable Union—beyond that dissolution."[4] Within a week the war spirit seized Midway and Milledgeville, where
the state legislature, then in session, invited several of Georgia's
most illustrious sons to address the body on the advisability of

---

1. *Oglethorpe University Catalogue*, 1860-1861, *passim*.
2. Starke, *Sidney Lanier*, 41.
3. Thalian Minutes, 75.
4. Clifford Lanier to Mary Lanier, Nov. 6, 1860. *Sidney Lanier*, cent. ed.,
   VII, 34 n.

secession. Among these was Robert Toombs, who advocated immediate disunion, calling attention to sectional discriminations such as tariffs and territorial restrictions, and concluded: "The time has come to redress these wrongs, and avert even greater evils of which they are but signs and symbols."[5] "I say," advised Thomas R. R. Cobb, "my voice is for *immediate*, unconditional secession. . . . I think I see in the future a gory head rise above our horizon. Its name is Civil War."[6]

When there was so much speech-making and excitement in Milledgeville, neither students nor faculty could keep away from the state capital that was so close at hand. As noted earlier, Dr. Talmage and Professor Lane accompanied a group of students to hear Ben Hill argue against immediate secession.[7] The night before, Oglethorpe boys listened to Alexander H. Stephens counsel delay and compromise:[8] "I am for exhausting all that patriotism demands before taking the last step. . . . I am, as you clearly perceive, for maintaining the Union as it is, if possible. I will exhaust every means thus to maintain it with an equality in it. My position, then, in conclusion, is for the maintenance of the honor, the rights, the equality, the security, and the glory in my native State in the Union if possible; but if these cannot be maintained in the Union, then I am for their maintenance at all hazards out of it. Next to the honor and glory of Georgia, the land of my birth, I hold the honor and glory of our common country."[9]

From the few surviving records, it seems that many, if not most, Oglethorpe students and faculty members favored Stephens's policy of hopeful waiting and reconciliation,[10] but gradually the minds of all, or nearly all, were changed. On December 20, 1860, South Carolina seceded from the Union, and four weeks later,

---

5. Ulrich B. Phillips, *The Life of Robert Toombs* (New York, 1913), 200.
6. Allen D. Candler, ed., *The Confederate Records of the State of Georgia* (5 vols., Atlanta, 1909-1911), I, 159, 182.
7. *Supra.*
8. Cf. *Sidney Lanier*, cent. ed., VII, 37.
9. Henry Cleveland, *Alexander H. Stephens, in Public and Private with Letters and Speeches* (Philadelphia, 1866), 711-712.
10. Cf. Beeson, *Sidney Lanier at Oglethorpe*, 30. See also *Sidney Lanier*, cent. ed., VII, 34 n.

on the following January 16, the convention of Georgia assembled in Milledgeville to consider the same course. The delegates were the ablest men in the state, several of whom Oglethorpe students had heard debate secession two months before. Robert Toombs and Thomas R. R. Cobb again urged immediate disunion, while Alexander H. Stephens and Ben Hill again pleaded for delay and reconciliation. The issue was brought to a head when Eugenius A. Nisbet, chairman of the Board of Trustees of Oglethorpe, introduced a resolution, stating "it is the right and duty of Georgia to secede from the present union," and recommended that a committee "be appointed by the Chair to report an ordinance to assert the right, and fulfill the obligation of the State of Georgia to secede. . . ."[11] The next day, Saturday, January 19, 1861, a test vote was taken on Nisbet's motion, and carried by a vote of 166 to 130.[12] By a later vote secession carried 208 to 89, and to prove that the state was a unit now that the act was passed, every delegate of the convention, including even Stephens and Hill, signed the resolution.[13]

As the proceedings of the convention were secret, Oglethorpe students and faculty members did not have the privilege of hearing the heated debates, as they had done in November, but many of them waited outside the capitol,[14] with hundreds of others who had assembled to learn the decision of the delegates.[15] When finally the news of the adoption of the secession ordinance reached the crowd, "there was an exultant shout," reported one newspaper, "and men breathed freer and looked nobler, and felt more like freemen, who had burst the shackles that had enslaved them for years. . . . The people shouted, the bells were rung, the cannon roared, the city was illuminated, and great was the rejoic-

---

11. *Journal of the Public and Secret Proceedings of the Convention of the People of Georgia* (Milledgeville, Ga., 1861), 15.
12. Candler, ed., *Confederate Records of Georgia*, I, 236.
13. *Ibid.*, 256; Avery, *History of Georgia*, 155-156.
14. Thalian Minutes, 25.
15. Percy Scott Flippin, *Herschel V. Johnson of Georgia, State Rights Unionist* (Richmond, Va., 1931), 190-191.

ing."[16] The secessionists were jubilant and in the evening a torch-light procession was climaxed by a festival of patriotic speeches.[17] Though it is not a matter of record, it is almost certain that the Oglethorpe boys entered into the spirit of the celebrations as heartily as anyone present.[18]

The Unionism that had prevailed among the students and faculty in the fall of 1860 soon vanished in this almost universal enthusiasm for a new age that was being inaugurated in the South. One Oglethorpe man dreamed that "the new Confederacy was to enter upon an era of prosperity such as no other nation, ancient or modern, had ever enjoyed, [and that] the city of Macon, his birthplace and home, was to become a great art-centre. Its streets were to be lined with marble statues, like unto Athens of old."[19] Furthermore he was "convinced of his ability to whip at least five Yankees." He was "also confident, not only that he personally could whip five Yankees, but *any* Southern boy could do it. The whole South was satisfied it could whip five Norths. The newspapers said we could do it; the preachers pronounced anathemas against the man that didn't believe we could do it; our old men said at the street corners, if they were young they could do it, and by the Eternal, they believed they could do it anyhow . . . ; the young men said they'd be blanked if they couldn't do it, and the young ladies said they wouldn't marry a man who couldn't do it."[20]

It was this state of public mind in the spring of 1861 that Sidney Lanier describes in *Tiger-Lilies*: "An afflatus of war was breathed upon us. Like a great wind, it drew on and blew upon men, women, and children. Its sound mingled with the solemnity of the church-organs and arose with the earnest words of preachers praying for guidance in the matter. It sighed in the half-breathed words of

16. Atlanta *Intelligencer*, Jan., 1862, quoted in Avery, *History of Georgia*, 155-156. Avery says "Atlanta *Intelligencer* one year later," which probably means Jan. 19 or 20, 1862. No file of this paper is known to exist for 1862.
17. Flippin, *Herschel V. Johnson*, 191.
18. *Infra.*
19. Northrup, *loc. cit.*, 303.
20. Mims, *Sidney Lanier*, 46.

sweethearts conditioning impatient lovers with war-services. It thundered splendidly in the impassioned appeals of orators to the people. It whistled through the streets, it stole in to the firesides, it clinked glasses in bar-rooms, it lifted the gray hairs of our wise men in conventions, it thrilled through the lectures in college halls, it rustled the thumbed book-leaves of the schoolrooms.

"This wind blew upon all the vanes of all the churches of the country, and turned them one way—toward war. It blew, and shook out, as if by magic, a flag whose devise was unknown to soldier or sailor before, but whose every flap and flutter made the blood bound in our veins.

"Who could have resisted the fair anticipations which the new war-tides brought? It arrayed the sanctity of a righteous cause in the brilliant trappings of military display; pleasing, so, the devout and the flippant which in various proportions are mixed elements in all men. It challenged the patriotism of the sober citizen, while it inflamed the dream of the statesman, ambitious for his country and for himself. It offered test to all allegiances and loyalties; of church, of state; of private loves, of public devotion; of personal consanguinity; of social ties. To obscurity it held out eminence; to poverty, wealth; to greed, a gorged maw; to speculation, legalized gambling; to patriotism, a country; to statesmanship, a government; to virtue, purity; and to love, what all love most desires—a field wherein to assert itself by action."[21]

Opportunity for action was not long in coming. On February 4, one month before Abraham Lincoln took office, a convention of the seceded states met at Montgomery, Alabama, and elected Jefferson Davis provisional President of the Confederate States of America and Alexander H. Stephens provisional Vice-President. Immediately after his inauguration on February 18, President Davis sent a committee to Washington to negotiate for the friendly adjustment of all questions with the government of the United States. But the efforts for peace were fruitless. When Lincoln assumed office, the seceded states had taken possession of all Federal forts and arsenals in their limits, except Fort Sumter and

21. *Tiger-Lilies* (New York, 1867), 119-120.

a few small coast defenses. After delaying and equivocating, Lincoln determined to reinforce Fort Sumter. Early in the morning of April 12 a Charleston battery fired the first shot—and the war began! The Oglethorpe campus had never before known the intense excitement that now seized it. Believing that the war would be over within three months and fearing that they would not have a part in it students began withdrawing from the University and volunteering for Confederate service.[22]

Some of the older boys organized a militia company, which they named the "University Guards." On May 1 the ladies of the community presented the Guards with a flag in a colorful ceremony in front of the Midway Female Academy. The company was attended by the Milledgeville Cavalry and a detachment of the Troup Artillery of Baldwin County. Dr. Nathaniel A. Pratt, professor of natural science at the University, delivered the presentation speech. Throwing aside the cool reasoning of a scientist, Dr. Pratt portrayed the darkness of the current dangers, which, however, he thought, were relieved "by the brightness of a just cause." He "deprecated overweening contempt, undue hatred, and revengeful feeling on the part of Southern men, and bade the company be calm, that they might strike truly and heavily on the day of battle." He insisted that "the essential prerequisite to soldierly excellence was manly virtue." Captain E. Postelle Cater, a member of the senior class and a native of South Carolina, accepted the flag "with a beautiful speech of thanks." In referring to Fort Sumter, he spoke of the dangers that brave men had suffered in his state "in preserving their flag from the polluting hands of enemies." He pledged that if it should ever become necessary, he and his company would either march to victory under their "hallowed" flag or "die wrapped in its folds."[23]

In view of the military excitement, the Trustees closed the University two months earlier than usual. On May 28, eighteen seniors assembled in the college chapel to receive their diplomas. For the first time in Oglethorpe's history commencement was not at-

---

22. Beeson, *Sidney Lanier at Oglethorpe*, 45.
23. The Macon *Daily Telegraph*, May 15, 1861. See also *Sidney Lanier*, cent. ed., V, 197-199.

tended by large crowds and the usual flow of oratory. There were no senior speeches, no music, none of those features that had previously made commencement "great." After Professor Pratt pronounced the invocation, Dr. Talmage addressed the senior class on their three-fold duties as citizens, scholars, and Christians. He alluded to the war and urged the graduating class to support the Confederacy and to maintain "our honor and rights."[24]

Fellow students bid a final farewell and hastened to volunteer for military service. Practically every graduating senior[25] and all except four juniors who were too young to serve enlisted in the Southern army.[26] The faculty was as patriotic as the students. On the day after commencement Dr. Talmage participated in a public meeting in Milledgeville called by Governor Brown, who asked for $1,000,000 from the citizens of Georgia to aid in defense of the Confederacy, $87,000 being the quota of Baldwin County. Dr. Talmage offered the invocation, and the audience sang the "National Hymn":

> God bless our Southern land!
> Guard our beloved land!
> God save the South!
> Make us victorious,
> Happy and glorious;
> Spread Thy Shield over us;
> God save the South!

In addressing the meeting, the University president proposed to become one of eighty-seven citizens to "subscribe $100 on the spot." Every farmer present subscribed, and Governor Brown gave $1,000.[27]

Another faculty member, Dr. Pratt, organized a militia company, the "Jordan Grays," named in honor of Lee Jordan, who generously bore the entire expense of equipping the volunteers. The company was mustered into the service of the state on November 28, 1861, and was immediately ordered to the coast

---

24. *Southern Recorder*, June 4, 1861; T. Minutes, 1875-70, p. 222.
25. Mims, *Sidney Lanier*, 47 n.
26. *Infra*, 106.
27. *Southern Recorder*, June 4 ,1861.

near Savannah. After a few months the Confederate government, recognizing Captain Pratt's scientific ability, detached him for service in the Niter and Mining Bureau at Augusta. As the chief scientific adviser of the Bureau, he investigated the natural resources of the South that could be used in the manufacture of war supplies, especially of gunpowder. He served in this capacity until the end of the war.[28]

His predecessor at Oglethorpe, Dr. James Woodrow, who had gone to the Columbia Theological Seminary in 1861, enlisted as a private, but before seeing actual military service, he was appointed head of the government plant for the manufacture of medicine in Columbia. As an expert chemist, he conducted the work with notable success until Sherman's army destroyed the city in February, 1865.[29]

In this work he was assisted by Dr. Joseph Le Conte, whom he had succeeded at Oglethorpe in 1853. Dr. Le Conte reported that he "was engaged in the manufacture on a large scale of many kinds of medicine, alcohol, nitrate of silver, chloroform, sulfuric ether, nitric ether, podophyllin etc. The whole army was supplied by this laboratory with all medicines, except those that could be had more easily by running the blockade." During the last year of the war Dr. Le Conte served as chemist in the Niter and Mining Bureau just as Dr. Pratt was doing. His new commission required him to visit niter deposits in South Carolina, Georgia, Alabama, and Tennessee, and the iron mines and blast furnaces at Shelbyville, Alabama.[30]

Young Tutor Lanier volunteered for service in June, 1861, and was sent immediately to join the Macon Volunteers, who had left Georgia for Norfolk, Virginia, on April 19. For the first year he considered the war a kind of grand lark, but in May, 1862, he experienced his baptism of fire at Drury Bluff, about seven miles south of Richmond on the James.[31] Just before this engagement, his brother Clifford, reaching the age of eighteen,

28. Northen, ed., *Men of Mark in Georgia*, V, 106.
29. Woodrow, *Dr. James Woodrow*, 20-21.
30. Armes, ed., *Autobiography of Joseph Le Conte*, 184.
31. Starke, *Sidney Lanier*, 44-45.

had withdrawn from Oglethorpe while still a sophomore, and enlisted in Sidney's regiment.[32] The two brothers soon saw war at its worst in the seven days' fighting around Richmond (June 26-July 2, 1862). Before the battle of Malvern Hill (July 1) the Confederates marched all night long through pouring rains and over muddy swampy roads. In August the regiment was ordered to Petersburg for rest, and here Sidney and Clifford enjoyed an inseparably close companionship in developing their minds and talents, which were already turning to literature and music. In 1863 the brothers obtained a transfer to the Mounted Signal Service. For their proficiency they were attached to the staff of Major General Samuel G. French. Sometimes in the evening Sidney and others would go to the quarters of the General and entertain him with music.[33]

The Laniers saw no more fighting until the two days' battle of Chancellorsville (May 2-3, 1864), but they sustained no wounds though nearly a fourth of the Confederate forces were lost. After Chancellorsville, they were ordered back to Fort Boykin on the James, where they resumed their duties as mounted scouts. Here they remained over a year.

In August, 1864, they were transferred to Wilmington, North Carolina, where Sidney was made a signal officer of the *Lucy*. November 2, his ship was captured in the Gulf Stream by the Federal Cruiser *Santiago-de-Cuba*, and he was taken prisoner to Fortress Monroe, then to Camp Hamilton, and finally to Point Lookout, Maryland, where he spent over three months of living hell, described in *Tiger-Lilies*. He was released near the end of February, 1865, and reached Macon on March 15, more nearly dead than alive.[34]

In the meanwhile his brother Clifford had become a signal officer on the *Talisman*, a blockade runner plying between Wilmington and Nassau. He made three exciting runs, but in Decem-

32. G. Prescott Atkinson, "Sidney Lanier," *Library of Southern Literature*, VII, 3021-3022.
33. Samuel G. French, *Two Wars: An Autobiography* (Nashville, Tenn., 1901), 157.
34. For the best treatment of Lanier in the war, see Starke, *Sidney Lanier*, 44-65.

ber, 1864, his vessel was wrecked and he was rescued by a Federal
schooner. He escaped to Cuba, where he heard of the capture of
Wilmington. He then ran the blockade to Galveston, Texas, and
after several weeks in that city, returned home two months after
Sidney had arrived.[35]

The one conspicuous example of an Oglethorpe man who failed
to choose the Confederate side was Milton Harlow Northrup,
principal of Midway Academy for Boys and an ex officio member
of the University faculty. A native of New York state and a
graduate of Hamilton College, he had come to Midway in 1860.
There he and Lanier occupied adjoining rooms at Ike Sherman's
boarding house and ate at the same table. Their mutual interest in
literature and music soon combined to weld a bond of friendship
that not even the bitterness of war could unbind. In 1861 Northrup reached his home in Syracuse with the greatest difficulty.
During the war a Northerner who escaped the South by running the blockade took back memories of the most enchanting
flute-playing he had ever heard. When Northrup overheard his
description of the music, he asked if the player was Sidney Lanier.
It was. This was the only news that Northrup heard of his Oglethorpe friend until the close of the war. After Lanier returned
home in 1865, he began a correspondence with Northrup that
lasted until the poet's death.[36]

The effects of the war upon the administration of the University were evident from the start. Following the early commencement in '61, the school reopened the first Tuesday in October, but with a greatly diminished enrollment.[37] By May, 1862,
many of the lower classmen and all four members of the senior
class had been called to Confederate service by the Conscript Act
of that year. Therefore the Trustees decided to close the University
on May 30. There were no commencement exercises. On the rec-
ommendation of the faculty, the four seniors were granted their
A.B. degrees *in absentia*, thus becoming the last graduating class
at Midway.[38]

---

35. *Ibid.*, 64-65.
36. *Ibid.*, 38-39, 44-45.
37. T. Minutes, 1835-70, p. 222.
38. *Ibid.*, 224; *Southern Recorder*, June 17, 1862.

In October of 1862, the University resumed exercises with the few students who were not of military age; but it was soon evident that thenceforth the college could be kept open only nominally. Recognizing the insecure position of the school, the three remaining faculty members—Talmage, Smith and Lane—agreed during the summer that they would "rely upon whatever their professorships might yield for their salaries" in the ensuing year.[39] But hardly had the fall term begun when the serious illness of Dr. Talmage took away his excellent leadership. Torn between love of his native North and his adopted South, he was seized with paralysis and convulsions. After each attack his mind was so clouded that it was necessary to put him in the nearby insane asylum. It was hoped that rest and treatment by his friend Dr. Thomas F. Green would restore the president to mental health, but no permanent improvement was noted.[40]

During the prolonged illness of Dr. Talmage, Professor Smith was named to act as head of the University. He performed the duties of the president until the college was closed by the war, but with no senior class and only a handful of boys too young or unfit for Confederate service his executive responsibilities could not have been great. Only one member of the faculty—Professor Lane—remained to assist him.[41]

The University was operated on this curtailed program throughout the school year, '62-'63, and was closed June 12, 1863. The following month the Trustees met and resolved that: "Exercises of the college be resumed on the 1st Tuesday in October next as usual."[42] But a few weeks before the fall term was to begin, the first fighting on Georgia soil occurred at Chickamauga in September, 1863. Theretofore the remoteness of the University from the scenes of battle had developed no war scares in Midway, but now that the conflict was so near, fear seized everyone. When the time for starting the fall term arrived, Oglethorpe

---

39. T. Minutes, 1835-70, p. 226.
40. *Ibid.*, 232, 238-239, 242; Wilson, *Necrology*, 290.
41. Allen, "Old Oglethorpe University," 72.
42. T. Minutes, 1835-70, p. 232.

was not reopened and it remained closed until after the war was ended.[43]

When the college closed, Professor Lane, though a native of New England, became a chaplain in the Army of Northern Virginia. He spent his time distributing Testaments in the hospitals and praying and talking with the wounded and dying. One day when he came to a Texas Ranger, wearing a blood clotted shirt, he asked the soldier if he wanted a Bible. The wounded man answered abruptly, "No, but I want a clean shirt." Dr. Lane took one of his own from his valise and put it on the Texan. The soldier was then glad to accept religious instruction, which led to his conversion. Dr. Lane continued such humble service until the end of the war.[44]

The gravity of the war was impressed on residents of Midway as Sherman's army neared Atlanta. Just before the battle of Kennesaw Mountain, in May, 1864, Captain F. W. Capers, superintendent of the Georgia Military Institute at Marietta, wrote to Dr. Talmage requesting the privilege of using the vacant college buildings as a hospital for the sick and disabled cadets, and as a place of refuge for the families of the officers. The request was cordially granted, and soon the college campus took on a military appearance.[45] The young ladies of Midway rejoiced to see the cadets, who though they were sick men, nevertheless were men, and they brought back some of the ardor of youth that had vanished when the students went away to fight.[46]

During the summer of 1864 the fighting around Atlanta kept the college community in a state of constant anxiety. Federal raiders were reported from time to time in Baldwin County, but they did no worse harm than steal a few livestock.[47] The Con-

43. The Trustee Minutes, 1835-70, show that the Trustees held no meeting. from July 21, 1863 (p. 231) until Sept. 6, 1865 (p. 234). The Thalian Minutes come to an abrupt conclusion when the last entry was made June 11, 1863.
44. *Entered into Rest June 19th, 1896, Rev. Charles Whitmarsh Lane, D.D.,* (Athens, Ga., n.d.), 2-3.
45. F. W. Capers to Dr. Talmage, May 24, 1864. Letter in possession of Miss Pauline McKinley, Milledgeville.
46. Manuscript Diary of Anna Maria Green Cook, 72, 82. In the possession of her daughter, Mrs. Addie Cook Proctor, of Midway.
47. *Ibid.,* 75.

federate victory in the first battle of Atlanta (July 22) naturally brought hope that Sherman's invasion of Georgia had failed and that the state capital would be spared, but the Gate City finally surrendered in September and the Federal army began its march to the sea on November 15.

The vanguard of Sherman's cavalry reached Milledgeville on Sunday, November 20, with a small body of not more than twenty horsemen. After lingering on the outskirts of the city until they were satisfied that there was no Confederate force within, they cut the telegraph wires and advanced through the streets with cocked pistols and carbines. This produced panic among the citizens, but little material damage resulted until Sherman himself arrived two days later. For the most part, the people of Milledgeville remained in their homes, but Governor Brown, the State officers, and the legislature, which was in session, fled when they learned that the Federal army was near.[48]

During the occupation by the invading army the city became one vast military camp. The Federals generally respected families in their homes, but they seized anything outside that they wanted or needed. Wooden fences were torn down for firewood, and gardens and private yards became highways for horses and soldiers. Corn, fodder, horses, mules, hogs, cattle, sheep, and poultry were taken for the use of the army, while slaves that could not be enticed or forced were impressed into military service. Yet with all the vandalism and robbing, only two or three private homes were burned, and they belonged to leading secessionists.[49]

Public property was not so spared. Sherman gave orders for the total destruction of the arsenal in the penitentiary and its contents, and of buildings that could be easily converted to war purposes. The Gordon Railroad was destroyed as far south as Midway, and from Gordon four miles north so that the college community was left without means of transportation and communication with the rest of the state.[50] However, none of the college

---

48. *Southern Recorder*, Dec. 20, 1864; Avery, *History of Georgia*, 307-311.
49. *Southern Recorder*, Dec. 20, 1864.
50. *Ibid.; Personal Memoirs of Gen. W. T. Sherman [by Himself]* (2 vols. New York, 1890), II, 190.

buildings or private homes were burned. The State Insane Asylum, less than a mile from the University, was in no way molested.[51]

When the Federal forces approached Midway, they noticed a yellow flag flying over Thalian Hall and the dormitories, indicating that they were being used for a hospital. The commanding officer of the Federals had a special interest in and respect for Oglethorpe. It happened that his brother, Warren W. W. Clay, had been graduated with first honors at the University in 1857. Though a Northerner, he had spoken in defense of slavery, and his oration attracted so much attention that Governor Herschel V. Johnson wished to have it published. In 1861 just before the war Clay died, and Dr. Talmage sent the mother of the youth a letter of consolation.

"Accept, my dear madam, my deep sympathy for you in your sad hour of bereavement, and my earnest prayer to our Heavenly Father, that he will give you grace to bear your trials. May our blessed Saviour, who is 'touched with the feeling of our infirmities' pour the oil of consolation into your wounded spirit. . . .

"I felt a very strong attachment for your son. His whole deportment during his residence here secured for him the confidence of the whole community and a strong band of friends. His intellect was of a high order; his habits of study were laborious; and consequently he made himself one of the best scholars in the institution. His conduct was so gentlemanly and uniformly correct; his disposition so amiable and his manners so exemplary and unblamable that he reconciliated the respect and affection of all with whom he associated, both fellow students and teachers."[52]

This letter naturally kindled a tender spark in the hearts of the bereaved family, and when the older brother, now in command of the 102nd Regiment, Illinois Volunteers, reached Milledgeville, he was eager to visit the college scenes where Warren Clay was graduated seven years before. Riding out to Midway with a small force, the Federal officer inquired if Dr. Talmage or

---

51. It has often been said that the college buildings were burned by Sherman's army. As an example see Eleanor Williams, *Ivan Allen, A Resourceful Citizen* (Atlanta, 1950), 90.
52. Hiland H. Clay, *Genealogy and History of the Clay Family* (n. p., 1916), 36, 70.

any of the professors were living near. He learned that the president was ill and all except Professor Smith were gone to the war. When he found this lone faculty member, the old man leaped with joy to find a friend in the invading army. He then took the officer to the classrooms where his brother had recited and into the auditorium where he had delivered his memorable address on slavery. The Northerner was noticeably moved and would allow no molestation of the college buildings.[53]

Back in Milledgeville the state capitol was not so respected. When the Confederate flag was hauled down and the Stars and Stripes raised, some of the Federal officers gathered in the Representatives hall, where Oglethorpe students and faculty members had heard secession debated. In a mock session the officers constituted themselves the General Assembly of Georgia and debated the ordinance of secession, which resulted in its repeal.[54] Though these frolics caused no destruction of property, the capitol was later dismantled and the official papers of the state were strewn over the floors. About a fourth of the volumes in the general library were taken away, but the most valuable law books, which were deposited in the insane asylum at Midway, were saved uninjured.[55] No books were reported stolen from the Oglethorpe library.[56]

The last of the Federal army departed on November 25, the right wing passing through the University grounds en route to Gordon. Everyone was jubilant over Sherman's leaving and was especially thankful that Midway and Milledgeville had been spared the fate of Atlanta. As compared with that city, the towns of Baldwin County had suffered nothing. But the losses were greater than was first supposed. Sherman left the towns without food or means of transportation so that appeals were made to Macon for help. But hardly was the army out of sight when the

---

53. Allen, "Old Oglethorpe University," 72-73.
54. Sherman, *Personal Memoirs*, II, 190. See also Diary of Mrs. Cook, 75.
55. *Southern Recorder*, Dec. 20, 1864; John H. Conley, *Catalogue of the Georgia State Library, 1869* (Atlanta, 1869), iii. See also Diary of Mrs. Cook, 93.
56. *Southern Recorder*, Dec. 20, 1864; Stacy, *Presbyterian Church in Georgia*, 123, 138.

people began expending their energy in repairing and clearing
the streets. Before Christmas trains were running from Macon
to Midway.[57] At this point passengers to Milledgeville and far-
ther northward found it necessary to hire coaches or wagons to
proceed. Midway, now being the terminus of the railroad, enjoyed a boom of prosperity. Coachmen and draymen, taking advantage of travelers, charged exorbitant prices.[58]

This prosperity was neither lasting nor widespread in the college town. On December 22 Sherman presented Savannah to
Lincoln as a Christmas gift,[59] and a month after Lee surrendered
at Appomattox, Federal troops were back in Baldwin County. On
May 9, 1865, Joseph E. Brown was arrested in the Executive Mansion by order of General J. H. Wilson, and was taken to Washington and there imprisoned though the Governor had surrendered
the state troops the week before and had received a parole that
protected him. When President Andrew Johnson learned that
Brown's parole had been violated, he released him and the Governor came home to tell the people of Georgia that the war was
over and the Confederacy had failed.[60]

Defeat for the Confederacy meant financial ruin for Oglethorpe. Its endowment, largely in Confederate notes and bonds,
was nearly worthless. Fortunately the good management of Colonel John Gresham, treasurer of the Georgia and Florida Synod,
had preserved a sum of $28,000; but the assets of the other two
synods, being all in Confederate securities, were no longer reck-
oned of value and were sealed up and deposited in the treasury.[61]

As a crowning blow of defeat came the death of President Talmage. He died at Midway on September 2, 1865, at the age of
sixty-seven. He was one of the most able men in the whole history
of higher education in Georgia and was perhaps the only one who
could have saved the University from its postwar troubles and
eventual ruin. Today he is almost forgotten, but while he lived,
he was one of the most beloved and most respected men in the

57. *Southern Recorder*, Dec. 20, 1864.
58. *Autobiography of Joseph Le Conte*, 201.
59. Avery, *History of Georgia*, 321.
60. Candler, ed., *Confederate Records of Georgia*, II, 884-892.
61. T. Minutes, 1835-70, p. 234; Stacy, *Presbyterian Church in Georgia*, 123.

state. The contemporary esteem of Dr. Talmage is revealed in the resolution of the Board of Trustees of Oglethorpe, adopted four days after his death:

At the breaking out of the late war, with an able corps of instructors, with classes numerically respectable and increasing, and with the confidence of the public, the University stood in the first rank of Denominational Institutions in the South. It had become a decided success, and was indebted in an eminent degree for its great usefulness to the ability, and indomitable energy of its *President*. In the recitation room he was apt in communicating knowledge, and in discipline paternal, yet firm, relying more upon appeals to a sense of character than the penal violation of law. He was patient, affable, vigilant and persistent. An accomplished classical scholar, and a finished rhetorician, he was a beautiful exemplar of polite literature. As such he became a model for the young men under his charge. Naturally he was a generous and magnanimous man. It is not surprising, therefore, that he inspired his character upon them. He was in the habit of devoting his long vacations to preaching excursions into the country; and wherever he went, at the seat of Government, in the towns and villages, before the Presbyteries and Synods, and through the religious and secular papers, he instantly pressed the claims of religious education, and of Oglethorpe University. Indeed, it is more than probable that excessive labor for a number of years contributed to the disease which finally closed his life . . . .

The loss of the mind of a man so great and so good, is one of the mysteries of Providence which inspires awe and trembling, and the solution of which, it were folly to undertake. We only know that the Lord of all the earth will do right, and that it is our duty, humbly to submit to the most inscrutable of His dispensations. He died suddenly and without pain; and whilst his death was a great loss to the Church, the College, and the country, it is to him ineffable gain. His work was done. God called him; and whilst we are bereaved, he is transferred to the upper Sanctuary. We rejoice in the conviction of his acceptance by God, through the merits of his Son. The fruits of his life are proofs quite sufficient for this conviction. His example lives, and we hope to emulate his virtues. . . .

Peace be still — he is not dead but sleepeth — his spirit is in the bosom of God, and his body shall rise again glorified at the last day.[62]

---

62. T. Minutes, 1835-70, pp. 242-243.

CHAPTER VIII

Reconstruction Worse Than War

BALDWIN County, and all Georgia as well, was in a near state of governmental, financial, and economic prostration in the summer of 1865. News of the surrenders of Robert E. Lee and Joe Johnston, coupled with the sudden termination of the war, brought all business to a dead rest in Milledgeville. The Confederate currency was immediately rendered valueless, and the merchants who had anything to sell shut up shop, or hid their wares out of sight, rather than accept the only medium of exchange that most Southerners had. The effect of this check upon the currency was to stop almost every kind of business. Men who had been hard workers all during the conflict became idlers and drones. The streets of the state capital were daily crowded with people, whose only occupation seemed to be to talk, to smoke (they could buy nothing to drink), and to while away their time.

The greatest evil, wrought by the stagnation in business and trade and the absence of an adequate currency, was that those who did not own farms or plantations could get nothing to eat. Farmers, like business men, refused to exchange their products for worthless money, and they were not disposed to barter. The chief problem of most housewives became that of finding food for their hungry children and themselves.[1] "Everybody in Milledgeville was poor, everybody had fought and lost; everybody had seen better days. The community felt the comradeship and solidarity that come from common disaster. All had trod, in blood and tears, the road of defeat."[2]

Early in May paroled veterans of Lee's and Johnston's armies began to trickle into Baldwin County. Of the hundreds who left

---

1. *Federal Union*, May 9, 1865.
2. William G. McAdoo, *Crowded Years* (Boston and New York, 1931), 10.

in '61 in high spirits and good health, hardly half returned to their homes. And of that number most were either sick or disabled by wounds. The men who had attended Oglethorpe had suffered as much as anyone. Two sons of Dr. Tomlinson Fort, Tomlinson Jr., of the class of '57, and John Porter, of the class of '60, came back from the war physically broken both by wounds and hardships of army life. Another son, George W. Fort, came home so badly shaken in body that he lived only a year.[3] The three sons of Miller Grieve suffered as much as the Fort boys. Fleming, John, and Miller, Jr.—all matriculates of Oglethorpe—served for the full duration of the war and returned to Milledgeville in poor health. John left the University to join the Confederate army in 1861. For a year he was confined at Fort Henry in Maryland, where he contracted tuberculosis from exposure and hardships of prison. After the war he was never able to work and died in 1874. Joseph B. Newell, who attended the University for awhile in 1851, but who received his medical degree from Jefferson College in Philadelphia, had raised a volunteer company and fought four years in the Army of Northern Virginia. He came home in the summer of '65 and died within a year. His brother, Tomlinson, of the class of '59, lost his left foot at Gettysburg, after which he spent eighteen months as a prisoner at Forts Henry and Delaware.

More fortunate were Edward Melvin Green of the class of '59; Henry Saye Orme of the class of '58; and the matriculates Edward Payson Lane, Thomas Howell Whitaker, and James Murf Whitaker, all of whom returned to Baldwin County with no loss of limb.[4] But these veterans—Oglethorpe men and others—were de-

---

3. John Porter Fort, *A Memorial and Personal Reminiscences* (New York, 1918), 38, 39. Just before Johnston surrendered at Goldsboro, Tomlinson, Jr., was stricken with an acute case of inflammatory rheumatism and had to be carried to escape capture. He was later sent to Raleigh in a wagon, where he partially recovered. When he finally reached home, he was pale and too weak to work. John Porter Fort got as far as Macon two days before Federal General John H. Wilson seized that city. He was suffering from incipient tuberculosis, but a year on his plantation in Sumter County restored him to his former strength and vigor.
4. Allen, "Old Oglethorpe University," 75, 77, 79, 89; Cook, *History of Baldwin County*, 348, 396, 472, 478.

spondent after Appomattox and hardly knew where or how to begin life anew. Naturally they talked much of the war and added to the general depression.

The woes of the people were increased by unprecedented weather. May of 1865 was cold and dry, and the sprouting gardens withered and died in the bud. The spring wheat was small and yielded only half a crop. Some farmers ploughed up their stunted corn and replanted it. Furthermore, peace meant freedom to the Negroes, who had worked the farms, and freedom to them meant idleness. Leaving their familiar rural scenes, they filled Milledgeville.[5] A rumor spread that the Federal government was preparing to seize the land of their former masters and appropriate it to the freedmen. When no seizures were made, the Negroes began taking anything and everything that was portable and useful to them. One citizen of Milledgeville complained, "If the Negroes go on stealing the fruits of our industry and frugality as they are doing now, in a short time there will be nothing left to feed either white man or negro, and the former will have to seek a new country where the works of his hands, at least, will be secure to him."[6]

On May 9, the day when General Wilson arrested Governor Brown and took him to a Washington jail, the Federal Army took over Baldwin County. The same day one of the local newspapers suspended operation, and the Confederate mail service came to an abrupt end. For a while the people were almost relegated to Rousseau's idealistic return to nature. With only one newspaper and that under Federal censorship, no mails, no railroad communications, and no state government, there existed a brief period of anarchy.[7] To relieve this chaotic condition, which prevailed not only in Baldwin County but throughout much of the South, President Andrew Johnson issued his famous proclamation on May 29 and began restoring the Southern states to their proper place in the Union. For provisional governor of Georgia he selected James Johnson, a strong Union man. A new constitution, abolishing slavery and denying the right of seces-

---

5. *Federal Union,* May 9, 1865.
6. *Ibid.,* Aug. 1, 1865.
7. *Ibid.,* May 9, 1865; Candler, ed., *Confederate Records of Georgia,* II, 884-886.

sion was adopted; the Confederate war debt was repudiated; and Charles J. Jenkins was elected governor; while Alexander H. Stephens and Herschel V. Johnson, whom Oglethorpe students before the war had greatly admired, were chosen United States senators. All of this transpired before the end of 1865.[8]

In the midst of all this confusion and revolutionary change, the Board of Trustees resolved to reopen Oglethorpe on October 4 and went so far as to advertise in the local newspapers that it would resume operation and offer instruction to all students in all the branches of a college education. Tuition was set at $20.00 per term in advance, or $60.00 per annum. Board was estimated at $4.00 per week, exclusive of washing, fuel, and lights. Special provisions were made for those wishing to pay in farm products.[9] The Trustees seemed oblivious of the dilapidated condition of the college buildings, which had been used as a Confederate hospital and were in bad need of repairs. Furthermore, no funds had been available for that purpose since 1861, and only two professors remained for instructional duty: Dr. Lane, who had just returned from war; and Dr. Smith, who had been in charge of the college since it had closed. As pointed out earlier, Dr. Talmage died in September; Dr. Pratt resigned during the war; and Tutor Lanier did not return to his post. In view of these discouraging circumstances, the Synod of Georgia ordered the college to be closed, but at a later meeting during the fall, fearing injury to the school property by further suspension, that body resolved to resume exercises January 16, 1866. Under an arrangement with Professors Smith and Lane instruction began on the appointed day with only twenty-five students in attendance in all classes.[10]

With these few students Oglethorpe completed the school term on June 15. There was no graduating class, but everyone wanted a commencement, so reminiscent of the pre-war days. There was no baccalaureate sermon as of old, but on Friday night the annual sophomore declamation contest was held in the chapel. Essays

---

8. Avery, *History of Georgia*, 335-352.
9. *Federal Union*, Sept. 12, 19, 26, 1865; *Southern Recorder*, Sept. 12, 19, 26, 1865.
10. *To the Trustees of Oglethorpe University*, a broadside in the possession of Miss Pauline McKinley, of Milledgeville.

were read, and a debate was held on the question, "Has African Slavery been an advantage to the Southern People?"[11] Everything was done to draw a large crowd, but a large crowd was not attracted. Like everything else in Baldwin County, commencement was only a reflection of what it had been before the war and its light had almost gone out.[12]

However dark things might be, the Trustees decided to resume the college in the fall. At their regular meeting in July they discussed the feasibility of removing Oglethorpe to some other point, where there was a better chance of reviving it. Earlier a committee had been appointed to ascertain the practicability of uniting the several Presbyterian colleges in the South and with the combined resources organizing a university upon the broadest plan of usefulness. The committee reported unfavorable to the union of the Southern colleges, and the Board resolved that for the time being, at least, Oglethorpe would remain at Midway and that every effort would be made "with the blessings of God to revive and sustain it" there.[13]

With renewed determination the University began the following October (1866), but the enrollment fell far short of what it had been before '61. As suggested earlier, many of the students who had gone away to fight for the Confederacy were now incapacitated with battle wounds or poor health. The people of Georgia appreciated what her sons had done to win Southern Independence, and before the end of the fall term the General Assembly of Georgia, as a token of the state's gratitude, passed a law providing an education, "free of charge for tuition, books, board and clothing" for all indigent and maimed veterans under thirty years of age, to be educated at the universities of Georgia, Mercer, Emory, and Oglethorpe and Bowdon College. The expenses were not to exceed $300.00 annually per student, in return for which, he pledged to teach within the state for a period of time equal to that in which he received aid.[14] The money that

11. *Federal Union*, June 22, 1866; *Southern Recorder*, June 12, 1866.
12. *Southern Recorder*, June 12, 1866.
13. T. Minutes, 1875-70, pp. 248 ff.
14. *Acts of the General Assembly of Georgia*, 1866, pp. 143, 144.

the University received from this source immediately alleviated its financial straits.

Many veterans took advantage of this opportunity and enrolled at once at Oglethorpe. At commencement in 1867 they took part in all of the exercises to the delight of the audience. They were more mature than most students who had attended in the ante bellum days, and the hardships of the war had made them more serious. Their conduct and influence on the younger boys changed the whole character of the student body. At commencement they were complimented on their good behavior, and the audience no longer had reason to complain of poor order, as they had so often done before '61. However, the attendance was only "respectable." "Where are the Alumni that came ever and anon to visit Alma Mater, and cheer the Faculty, students and friends?" asked one of the Trustees.[15] He did not answer, but many of Oglethorpe's sons were dead, more were wounded and sick, and nearly all were too poor to travel far just to see the reflected light of former days.

National Independence Day had once meant much to Oglethorpe students, but the war changed that also. In 1866 a citizen of Milledgeville sighed, "To-morrow is the famous 4th of July. It used to be a big day with us, when our boys had pretty uniforms and flashing guns and swords to go a mustering in—but the boys who used to carry them are sleeping under the sod—and the principles they made such a noise about are as dead as they are. The U. S. Congress has decided that our boys shall not serve in the Army or Navy of the U. S. any more—what use then for us to go a sogering on the 4th!"[16] Before the time for another celebration, Georgia was no longer a state in the Union, but merely a part of Military District Number 3 under the autocratic rule of General John D. Pope. The glamour of the Fourth of July had lost its meaning by what had transpired in the spring of 1867. President Johnson's plan of reconstruction was rejected by Congressmen, who formed their own plan, which the Southern states refused to accept. The Congress restored military rule much as

---

15. *Federal Union*, July 2, 1867.
16. *Ibid.*, July 3, 1866.

it had been in March, 1865, when the Confederacy had collapsed.[17] The humiliation of the South was now complete. How could Southerners celebrate independence when they were ruled by a Federal army? In 1867 and for several years thereafter, the Glorious Fourth was passed unobserved both at Oglethorpe and generally throughout Georgia. At the University there was no speaking, no picnic, no parade; and consciously no mention was made of the day.[18]

Before Georgia could be restored to the Union, the Congressional Acts of March, 1867, provided for the remaking of the state through a new electorate, which would include the Negroes and would exclude the most capable and respected leaders among the whites; and for a new constitution that would insure the civil and political rights of freedmen. The delegates to the constitutional convention met in the pushy city of Atlanta and enjoyed themselves so well that they made it the capital of the state.[19] This was a crippling blow to Milledgeville, from which it has never recovered. William Gibbs McAdoo, who was then too young to attend Oglethorpe, but who was a pupil at Midway Academy, later described the old capital realistically: "Nothing of importance was left in Milledgeville but an insane asylum and the state penitentiary. The town had a dejected, grass-grown appearance. In its center stood the abandoned capitol building, a solemn, owl-like structure. Its steps were littered with trash, and many of its windows were broken.

"In the dusty streets men pitched horseshoes and talked of the past. Nailed on the doorways were the signs of innumerable lawyers who had done very well while Milledgeville contained the authority and prestige of the state. Now that the capital was gone, they fluttered like dying leaves."[20]

The loss of the state government renewed agitation to remove the University to a more favorable location. The first legislature that met in Atlanta was composed of scalawags, carpetbaggers,

---

17. Avery, *History of Georgia*, 351-359.
18. The *Federal Union* and *Southern Recorder* make no mention of the Fourth in July, 1867, 1868, 1869.
19. E. Merton Coulter, *Georgia: A Short History* (Chapel Hill, 1947), 367-368.
20. McAdoo, *Crowded Years*, 12.

Negroes, and a few conservatives. On March 19, 1869, they discontinued aid to Georgia's maimed veterans, leaving them and Oglethorpe in financial distress.[21] Thus the reconstruction government dealt the *coup de grace* to the expiring University. With the veterans' support removed and the state government in Atlanta, everyone except a few people in Baldwin County despaired of ever seeing Oglethorpe revived at the old location. At the annual meeting of the Alabama Synod in 1869, Professor Smith spoke in behalf of the people of Midway and Milledgeville with reference to retaining the University in Baldwin County. The Alabama Presbyterians would not heed his appeal[22] and went so far as to pass a resolution "never to help the college unless it was removed."[23] This was so discouraging to Professor Smith that he resigned.

Professor Lane did his bit to keep Oglethorpe at Midway. To arouse popular interest, in January, 1869, (at the same time that the reconstruction legislature met in Atlanta), he began a series of lectures on botany, open to the public, in connection with his classes in the University. He illustrated his discourses by three large microscopes and used Alphonso Wood's *Botany* as a text book. He explained that he selected this book because "it is not *sectional*. It embraces in its description the gorgeous and magnificent vegetation of the Southern States." But not even an appeal to Southern patriotism attracted much interest either in the lectures or the University.[24] Dr. Lane resigned at the end of the school year, not because he had failed to arouse public appreciation, but to give full time to the ministry in which he was to serve for over a quarter of a century.[25]

Dr. Lane's and Dr. Smith's withdrawal left only one faculty member at Oglethorpe, Dr. Sylvanus Bates, professor of ancient languages. The University needed a president and that at once. Since the death of Dr. Talmage, Dr. Smith had acted in that ca-

21. *Acts of the General Assembly of Georgia*, 1869, p. 22.
22. An unidentified newsclipping in the possession of Miss Pauline McKinley.
23. Minutes of the Executive Committee of Oglethorpe University, 42. These manuscript minutes also are in the possession of Miss McKinley.
24. *Federal Union*, Jan. 19, Feb. 2, Mar. 2, Apr. 6, 1869.
25. Allen, "Old Oglethorpe University," 56.

pacity. In 1866 the Trustees elected Dr. Joseph C. Stiles, one of Georgia's leading Presbyterian ministers, to the presidency, but he declined. The next year they named Dr. Samuel J. Baird, upon condition that the University be removed, but when no action was taken to secure a new location, it became necessary to find another head for the school. A year later (1868) Judge John A. Ingles was chosen president, but he also refused the position. Finally Dr. William M. Cunningham, pastor of the La Grange Presbyterian Church, was chosen, and he accepted in November, 1869, but died within four months, in March, 1870.[26]

Disaster was heaped upon disaster. Shortly before Dr. Cunningham accepted the presidency, the Midway home of Professor Bates was completely destroyed by fire. The blaze broke out on the roof, and so high was the wind and so dry the shingles that the flames could not be extinguished. All that was saved was a considerable part of the household furniture. The violence of the wind imperilled the whole college community and actually set fire to the outbuildings of Colonel William Gibbs McAdoo, Sr., (father of the future Secretary of Treasury). The promptness of the Colonel in ascending the roof enabled him to put out the flames with his own hands. This quick action brought the fire under control before it reached other University buildings. The dwelling of Professor Bates was a part of the Oglethorpe property and was a total loss.[27]

Before another month had passed, the Trustees finally voted to remove the University. Earlier in the year they had discussed the question, but being equally divided they agreed to leave the decision to the three controlling synods and to abide by the action of the majority. As already related, Alabama refused further aid unless a new location was found. South Carolina voted to "leave it to the Synod of Georgia."[28] The Synod of Georgia and Florida that met in Tallahassee decided by the close vote of 26 to 22, to remove the University and to accept from the city of Atlanta a proposition which would fur-

26. T. Minutes, 1835-70, pp. 272, 282; *Federal Union*, Mar. 9, 1870.
27. *Federal Union*, Nov. 9, 1869.
28. Minutes of the Executive Committee, 42.

nish $40,000.00 toward its endowment. Some of the Trustees understood that Atlanta was offering also ten acres of land for a building site. Among them was Dr. James Stacy, who voted in the negative "from the deep conviction that removal would only sound the death knell of the Institution, as to his mind, it was a question of endowment, and not of location."[29] He thus showed himself one of the few disputants who clearly understood the basic trouble of Oglethorpe University. It seems extremely likely that Oglethorpe would have survived at Midway had the Trustees patiently waited until the economic crisis of reconstruction had passed. Emory College remained at Oxford until 1914 before it began removal to Atlanta and it was not established on its new campus until the end of World War I. Since then, it has become the best denominational school in the state and one of the greatest in the South.

Shortly before Dr. Cunningham's death the Trustees urged him to visit as many cities as possible to awaken interest in the University. Besides Atlanta, Macon made strong claims and proposed enticing inducements for its transfer to that city. La Grange was also in nomination, and offered to put "Brownwood Institute" in readiness within sixty days to accommodate 150 boarding students. Nearly 40 acres of land was also included.[30] But Atlanta put in the strongest bid of all.

On February 3, 1870, a citizens' meeting was held in the city hall to discuss plans for raising the $40,000.00 for removing Oglethorpe to Atlanta. Dr. Cunningham was invited to be the principal speaker. He set forth in terse and forcible language the peculiar advantages to be derived from locating the college in Atlanta both to the city and to the institution. First he emphasized that it was the desire of the Presbyterian Church to establish "not an academy, not a university, but a *first class college.*" Then he demonstrated "by facts and figures that the college would bring in annually, over $100,000.00 to the city," and add materially to the population of Atlanta. Finally he argued that the

29. Stacy, *Presbyterian Church in Georgia*, 126.
30. An unidentified newsclipping in the possession of Miss McKinley.

presence of a man's college would call for the establishment of a "first class female college" in the city.

"Citizens of Atlanta," he pleaded, "you need a college—you need one *now*. Before many years you will be convinced of the necessity. We now offer to endow and sustain a good college in your midst, if you will provide for us a *home*. Decline the offer, and you will soon be compelled to provide not only this home that we ask, but to furnish endowments, libraries, &c., at a cost of at least *one hundred and fifty thousand dollars*; and then have no pledged support from the country around. It is best to raise *forty thousand* for Oglethorpe, with the patronage it will bring, than expend *two hundred thousand* for an Atlanta college with no pledged support from abroad."[31]

The audience was impressed with Dr. Cunningham's plea and passed a resolution expressing the desire that an effort should be made at once to raise the necessary funds to bring the college to Atlanta and an Executive Committee of eleven prominent citizens were chosen to make arrangements and to secure the required sum.[32]

The Committee began at once to raise the necessary $40,000.00. Because of the post-war hard times, money was scarce and after four weeks, less than $15,000.00 had been subscribed. To prod those who had not contributed, the *Weekly Atlanta Intelligencer* urged: "We hope that the committee will diligently work, and use every effort to raise the amount required. We have too much at stake in this issue to admit of delay. We repeat what we have said on former occasions, that many other cities would gladly accept the boon which has been offered to us. It would be a proud triumph to them, to do what Atlanta had failed to do in this behalf. We say, wake up, and go to work bright and early, and raise the required amount of money."[33]

When the Trustees met at Macon, on March 31, 1870, Colonels

31. *The Weekly Atlanta Intelligencer*, Feb. 9, 1870.
32. *Ibid.* The committee included S. B. Hoyt, Col. E. Y. Clarke, Col. James M. Ball, John H. James, Lewis Schofield, Col. L. P. Grant, E. E. Rawson, Capt. W. G. Newman, W. A. Moore, W. McNaught, and Col. George W. Adair.
33. March 2, 1870.

L. P. Grant and E. Y. Clarke, members of the Executive Committee, were present to speak in behalf of the citizens of Atlanta. They submitted in writing a plan setting forth the following proposal: The city gave ten acres of land known as the "Fair Ground" valued at $12,000.00; the citizens of the south side of Atlanta subscribed $12,000.00, upon condition that the campus be located on McDonough Street; and the population at large contributed almost $16,000.00. The Trustees felt that Atlanta had "substantially complied" with the conditions and resolved to remove the University as soon as possible.[34]

The people of Atlanta rejoiced that a new college was established in their midst. Two months before the fall term began in 1870, the *Weekly Intelligencer* noted: "Oglethorpe locates here and will doubtless be a great blessing to the young men of the city, State and country—a radiating center of scientific and religious light, an honor, and an ornament of the noble church that founded and fosters her—her sons a light and blessing wherever found. . . . The Presbyterian church is a sufficient guaranty to all, of the wisdom of her Board of Trustees, ability of her Faculty, thoroughness of her education. Her works shall praise her, her impress on the current and coming generations be grand, her future bright, her blessings many."[35]

As soon as the Trustees decided definitely to locate Oglethorpe in Atlanta, the question arose what they should do with the property at Midway. They appointed a committee to study the matter and to report to the board at the meeting in June, 1870, when final decision was made to remove the University. The committee stated in their report that the University owned fifty acres of land, including some vacant lots and the campus, on which were the dilapidated college buildings, all of which was estimated to be worth $70,000; but that it would bring only a trifle of that sum. They thought it would be wrong to "throw away" what had cost so much. They therefore recommended that the Trustees convey all the real estate belonging to Oglethorpe at Midway to Thomas T. Windsor, Elder in the Milledge-

---

34. Minutes of the Executive Committee, 42.
35. August 3, 1870.

ville Presbyterian Church, in trust, who in turn should "convey to such seven other Trustees as might be in ten days elected" by the church,[36] for the purpose of establishing a high school upon the old campus. The transfer of the property was upon condition that it would revert to the Trustees of Oglethorpe if the Milledgeville church failed to sustain a school for two years. The Trustees of the University accepted the recommendations of the committee, and the real estate was immediately transferred under the condition aforesaid.[37]

Under this arrangement the "Milledgeville Presbyterian Church High School" began operation the following fall, with Professor Smith as principal.[38] In connection with the high school, a grammar school and primary grades were also conducted. One little fellow, aged seven, named William Gibbs McAdoo, began his quest for learning here. He must have got a good foundation, for he went far in the world. After he served as Secretary of the Treasury during World War I, he came back to Midway and joyfully reviewed the scenes of his happy childhood.[39]

After two years the school was closed, when Dr. Smith resigned and moved to Macon, where he spent the last few months of his life and died May 23, 1873.[40] The property at Midway was now again unused either as a college or a preparatory school. At the meeting of the Synod in the fall, 1872, that body resolved to establish "a school like Rugby, or Eton in England, between a Common school and College" on the old Oglethorpe campus. A committee was appointed "to consider and perfect the scheme at the next Synod."[41]

In 1873 the committee reported that because of opposition to ecclesiastical control of educational institutions, they proposed

---

36. Minutes of Executive Committee, 43. The committee elected by the Church were: Dr. Samuel G. White, Dr. George D. Case, Dr. William H. Hall, Randolph H. Ramsay, John A. Orme, William McKinley, and Lafayette Carrington. The last two were elected president and secretary respectively.
37. T. Minutes, 1835-70, p. 291.
38. *Federal Union*, Nov. 22, 1870.
39. Information furnished writer by old residents of Midway.
40. Allen, "History of Old Oglethorpe," 62.
41. *Minutes of the Synod of Georgia*, quoted in Stacy, *Presbyterian Church in Georgia*, 136.

to establish "the Talmage High School" and place it entirely under the control of a Board of Trustees. The Synod would retain only power "to appoint a new Board of Trustees should the Board at any time become extinct." The Talmage School began in September, 1874, but it soon proved a failure and was abandoned.[42]

The college buildings, now unused and neglected, hastened to decay and ruin. Central Hall, once the finest structure on any campus in Georgia, was left open, and birds built their nests in it and roosted in the class rooms. Goats wandered in and climbed the stairs leading to the belfry. As they nibbled on the rope hanging from the bell, its peals filled the air and reminded old Midway residents of the days when the ringing called Oglethorpe boys to their studies or to prayers. The small dormitories were one by one dismantled and carried away by unauthorized persons, probably for fire wood, until only one remained. By very questionable legal casuistry, the Trustees of the Milledgeville Presbyterian Church, to prevent further depredation, obtained an order from the Superior Court of Baldwin County by which the remaining property was sold for the benefit of that religious body.[43] Central Hall was torn down and its materials were bought by the State to be used in the construction of an addition to the T. O. Powell Building.[44] Today only Midway Chapel, Thalian Hall, and one of the wooden dormitories still stand. An Oglethorpe alumnus once bewailed the fate of his Alma Mater in this sad, but realistic language:

> Thus scattered to the four winds of heaven, this institution, this growing pride of the Presbyterian Church, finishes her career in disintegration and ruin, and now lies leveled in the dust, her halls deserted, her altars broken down, her fires gone out, and not a single vestige left; only her sons to tell of her former greatness, and shed bitter tears over her manifold miseries![45]

---

42. *Ibid.*, 137; *Minutes of Executive Committee*, 44.
43. Stacy, *Presbyterian Church in Georgia*, 137.
44. Cook, *History of Baldwin County*, 76. The high columns supporting the porch of the T. O. Powell Building and the front steps are said to be those of Central Hall. *Ibid.* Many old residents of Midway furnished the writer this information.
45. Stacy, *Presbyterian Church in Georgia*, 138.

CHAPTER IX

A Real University -- That Failed

O N October 4, 1870, Oglethorpe University opened in Atlanta with a corps of five professors in the college, six instructors in the law department, and three teachers in the University High School; and with ambitious plans already formulated for a medical college, a commercial department, and a civil engineering school.[1] When Dr. Cunningham had spoken before the citizens of Atlanta in February of that year, he had planned to establish "a first class college" and nothing more, but, after his death, the Trustees conceived grander ideas. Oglethorpe at Midway had never been a university in any sense except in name, but it had been a good college of as high standards as any other in the state. Its students had been treated not as young gentlemen, but as irresponsible boys who had to be governed by strict rules and regulations. It had well prepared its graduates to take their places in the society of the Old South, but the New South required more than the kind of education afforded in a small classical college.

In 1870 the prostrate South was slowly becoming adjusted to the new order and was beginning to look up again and call the land her own. No other state in the Confederacy had suffered more than Georgia during the war, and Atlanta had been hit harder than any other city in the state. Before Sherman started his famous march to the sea on November 15, 1864, his vandals had set fire to Atlanta and the flames entirely destroyed fully one half of the business section and every institution of learning except the Medical College as well as several of the churches. The influence of the Reverend Thomas O'Reilly had persuaded his fellow Catholics in the Federal army to spare his new church and rectory.

---

1. *Weekly Atlanta Intelligencer*, Nov. 2, 1870; John Stainback Wilson, *Atlanta As It Is* (New York, 1871), 35-37.

In saving the Catholic property from destruction, the Federals left Trinity Methodist, Second Baptist, and Second Presbyterian unharmed, which were hard by. A half mile north the Masonic Hall and a cluster of buildings in its neighborhood had been spared by the mystic signs and symbols of the fraternity, but all told less than five hundred houses in the entire city had survived the conflagration.[2]

Hardly had Sherman left the ruins of Atlanta when its citizens began to return, ready to repair and rebuild. So anxious were the homeless to find places to live, some families were housed in old freight cars; some used discarded army tents, while others were sheltered by scraps of old metal roofing nailed to a slight framework of timber. So fast did the Atlantans return that by 1866 the population was estimated at 20,000—more than it had ever been before the war. In 1870 when Oglethorpe began the fall term the United States census showed 21,789.[3]

The Trustees could hardly have chosen a new site for the University more unlike Milledgeville than the bustling, hustling city of Atlanta. Though it had been burned to the ground, it was quickly rising again from the ashes—'Resurgens' became its motto —and was too busy to weep over its recent fate. Milledgeville, which had suffered little physical damage in the war, was crushed by the outcome of the conflict and has ever since bewailed the loss of its former importance when it was capital of the state. Milledgeville looked to the past and typified the Old South. Atlanta looked to the future and was the very embodiment of the spirit of the New South.

In 1870 its real estate value was nearly $10,000,000 and the amount of goods sold reached a figure $3,000,000 higher. It boasted of having 875 licensed businesses, which included 400 retail stores, 50 liquor saloons, 28 butchers, 150 hackmen and draymen, 17 insurance agents, 9 printing offices, 15 contractors, 3 theatres, 5 hotels, 8 banks, 5 real estate agents, 4 bookstores, etc.

---

2. Report of General W. P. Howard to Governor Brown in Walter G. Cooper, *Official History of Fulton County* (Atlanta, 1934), 182-185.
3. Wilson, *Atlanta As It Is*, 9-10; Kate Massey, "A Picture of Atlanta in the Late Sixties," *Atlanta Historical Bulletin*, V, 1 (Jan., 1940), 34.

Besides these it had candy, soap, cracker, hoop-skirt, and ice "manufacturies." With no less than six incoming railroads, Atlanta was the largest center of transportation in the Southeast and proudly called itself the "Gate City." Everywhere the sound of hammers and saws told the story of costly buildings being erected, of real estate subdivisions expanding into the suburbs, and of millions of dollars being added to the city tax assessments. Everyone was making money and expecting to make more; the losses of war were forgotten in the hard work of rebuilding; and the puff of hundreds of locomotives and the clink of dollars muffled the cry of religion and the call for education.[4]

Oglethorpe must expand with Atlanta, must offer something for the advancement of learning in the wild scramble for wealth, in short must become a *real university* to serve this foremost city of the New South. On the same day when the Trustees chose Atlanta for the place of removal, they elected Dr. David Wills, a prominent Presbyterian minister, to be president of Oglethorpe.[5] Like Atlanta he was young, vigorous, and progressive. A native of Tennessee and a graduate of Tusculum College, he had finished his theological studies at the seminary in Columbia, South Carolina. In 1851 he was ordained and installed as pastor of the First Presbyterian Church at Laurens. While he served there, the Laurensville Female College was founded near his church, and he became its president in 1857. In 1860 he came to Georgia to be pastor of the First Presbyterian Church at Macon.[6] Because of his interest in education, he was elected to the Board of Trustees of Oglethorpe, and in recognition of his scholarship and service to the University he was honored with a D.D. degree in 1866.[7] He had other qualifications that fitted him to be an educational administrator. Physically he was tall and dignified in appearance, with a bearing that commanded respect. Like most

---

4. Wilson, *Atlanta As It Is*, 9-10, 49-50.
5. T. Minutes, 1835-70, p. 285.
6. Louis C. LaMotte, *Colored Light: The Story of the Influence of Columbia Theological Seminary* (Richmond, Va., 1937), 122-123, 302; F. D. Jones and W. H. Mills, *History of the Presbyterian Church in South Carolina since 1850* (Columbia, 1926), 1015.
7. T. Minutes, 1835-70, p. 255.

Presbyterian ministers of that day, he was a learned man, and he had developed his own ideas of what and how a university should teach.[8]

He held that the final objective of all learning was moral excellence. To know and to do the will of God was the chief business of everyone, especially of the educated. In addressing the graduating class in 1872, he paraphrased the Bible: "Fear God and keep His commandments, for that is the whole duty of man." Subordinate to this aim of education, but directed toward it, was scholarly attainment. "Drink deep or touch not the Pierian spring," he would advise his students. A thorough scholar himself, an eloquent orator, and a deep theologian, he had no patience with shallow education, and he warned Oglethorpe men against superficiality in their studies.[9]

To achieve high scholastic standards in the University, he began, with the approval and help of the Trustees, by selecting the best faculty that he could bring together. Not one of those who had taught at Midway removed with the University. Dr. Smith was elected professor of belles lettres and sacred literature, but he declined and remained on the old campus to head the high school. Professor Bates was deputed to collect the books in the library and the scientific apparatus and send them to Atlanta, and was elected to teach in the new University. He accepted the position, but resigned before the school was opened. Thus Dr. Wills was able to begin with a clean slate.[10]

In nothing that he undertook did he demonstrate his ability as an educator more strikingly than in the choice of the faculty. Every member at the time of his election was undistinguished and most of them were comparatively young men, but all were destined to make great contributions to the history of education in Georgia and the South. To take the place of the two professors who refused to remove with the University to Atlanta, two alumni of Oglethorpe, Donald Fraser, of the class of '48, and

---

8. Wilson, *Atlanta As It Is*, 36.
9. *Atlanta Constitution*, July 6, 1872.
10. Trustee Minutes of Oglethorpe University, 1870-87, pp. 14-15, 18. These minutes are kept in the vault of the new Oglethorpe in Atlanta.

Benjamin T. Hunter, of the class of '57, were asked to join the new faculty.

Professor Fraser was especially beloved by the Presbyterians of Georgia and became very popular with his students. He was a native of Liberty County, Georgia, and both his parents were of Puritan ancestry and faith. Thus he was reared in a home of religious zeal and fervor. At eighteen he was received into the famous Midway Church and immediately he determined to become a minister of the gospel. With that end in view he entered Oglethorpe in January, 1847, and was graduated with an A.B. degree in November, 1848. He then attended the Theological Seminary in Columbia, South Carolina. After graduation he served as pastor of churches first in Liberty County and later in Florida. In 1861 he joined the Confederate army and was made chaplain of the Second Florida Regiment. After the war he continued his ministerial duties until he was elected professor of ancient languages at Oglethorpe.[11]

As a teacher—*non fit sed nascitur*—he had the gift of imparting knowledge so attractively that he made Greek and Latin interesting to his students. While he taught at Oglethorpe, he and his family boarded at the Calico House, the home of one of his students, Piromis H. Bell. The professor generally sat at the head of the table. Sixty years later Bell wrote of Fraser: "I remember him as my teacher and as a most jovial and good natured Presbyterian divine. He generally led the conversation at this table, where were often seated more than thirty persons. I have seen him call the attention of all present to his plate well filled with hominy, or 'grits,' and vigorously stirring the viand, round and round with his fork, announce that this stirring made the 'grits' taste better. He often kept the table in roars of laughter."[12] Such a pleasant personality made him a favorite among the Oglethorpe students. He taught at the University until it was finally

---

11. Stacy, *History of Midway Congregational Church*, 121.
12. Piromis H. Bell, "The Calico House," *Atlanta Historical Bulletin*, I, 3 (May, 1930), 33-34. Mr. Bell is the only living person who attended Oglethorpe in 1870-1872. He is 93 years old and lives on Route 1, Decatur, Ga. He has furnished the present writer much information about Oglethorpe for this period.

closed and then he opened the Donald Fraser High School in DeKalb County, which is famous in Georgia history.[13]

Though nearly ten years younger than Professor Fraser, Professor Hunter was equally as capable both as a teacher and a scholar. In many respects the careers of the two men were very similar. A native of South Carolina, Hunter, like Fraser, was reared by pious Presbyterian parents, and early in life joined the church and decided to be a minister. To prepare himself, he, too, enrolled at Oglethorpe when he was about eighteen and was graduated with an A.B. degree in 1857. Next he attended the Columbia Theological Seminary and finished his course in 1860. That year he was ordained, but his plans for the ministry were interrupted by the war.[14] After 1865 he and W. W. Lumpkin conducted a high school on the campus of the University of Georgia, which was nicknamed "Rock College." As many of the veterans who were then attending school were unprepared for college work, most of them who entered the State University were required first to study under Professors Hunter and Lumpkin. For a while there were more students at Rock College than at the University, but in March, 1869, when the legislature withdrew financial aid of $300.00 per year, the veterans and the "College" were left in distress, just as they were at Oglethorpe. The decrease in attendance made it necessary for Professor Hunter to seek a new position.[15] Fortunately for Oglethorpe, he was available in the fall of 1870, and the Trustees elected him, with the recommendation of Dr. Wills, professor of physical science.[16]

Like Professor Fraser, Professor Hunter understood the psychology of young men. At "Rock College" most of his students were maimed or in some way disabled by the war. He and his co-teacher, W. W. Lumpkin, were most successful in training these veterans, some of whom became influential in later years.[17] At Oglethorpe Professor Hunter continued the good work of

---

13. Mr. Bell's information.
14. La Motte, *Colored Light*, p. 304.
15. Augustus L. Hull, *Annals of Athens* (Athens, 1906), 380; Coulter, *College Life*, 333.
16. T. Minutes, 1870-87, p. 14.
17. Hull, *Annals of Athens*, 380.

training young men, but resigned after just one year to go back to Athens to be the first president of the Georgia Industrial College.[18]

Destined to greater distinction in the history of Georgia education than either Fraser or Hunter was Gustavus John Orr, professor of mathematics at Oglethorpe from October, 1870, until January, 1872. Like Hunter, he was a native of South Carolina, but he came to Georgia as a child when his family moved to Jackson County. In 1844 he was graduated from Emory College and he made plans to study law in the office of his friend, Basil Hallam Overby. Because of financial necessity until he could be admitted to the bar, he accepted the principalship of the Jefferson Academy in his home county. This decision was important not only in the life of Orr, but also in the history of Georgia education. A year later he was made professor of mathematics at Emory College and taught there until 1868 when he resigned to become president of the Southern Masonic Female College at Covington, Georgia. He held this position until he accepted a professorship at Oglethorpe. After he had taught little more than a year in the University, Governor James M. Smith appointed him to the office of State School Commissioner. The public schools of Georgia had been established only two years when he accepted this position and in the last fifteen years of his life he became the greatest administrator ever to hold that office. He attracted nation-wide attention. In 1882 Woodrow Wilson, who was then a young attorney in Atlanta, listened admiringly as Orr pleaded before the state legislature for funds for the education of both whites and blacks. At the time of his death on December 11, 1887, Orr had earned the title "the father of the common school system in Georgia."[19]

The youngest member of the faculty was Walter Le Conte Stevens, a nephew of Professor Joseph Le Conte, who had taught at the University when it was at Midway. Stevens was born in Gordon County, Georgia, but grew up in Liberty County, where

---

18. Trustee Minutes of Oglethorpe University, 1870-1887, p. 36.
19. Dorothy Orr, *A History of Education in Georgia* (Chapel Hill, 1950), 406-407.

the effect of his Puritan maternal ancestry was strong in forming his character. His father "was a worthy and cultivated man and a successful physician." His mother was of an artistic nature, with "clear, vigorous and incisive" mental powers. She was deeply religious and did much home missionary work among the slaves. As a result of exposure in this endeavor, she contracted bronchitis and died in 1866 when Walter was nineteen years old. Dr. Stevens had already died, but the youth though deprived of both parents was able to enter the University of South Carolina, and was graduated in 1868. In 1870 when he was elected to teach at Oglethorpe he was only twenty-three years old, but in spite of his youth he was made professor of chemistry and thus began his distinguished career that lasted nearly sixty years. He remained at Oglethorpe until it was closed in 1872. Thereafter he taught successively at Chatham Academy, in Savannah; Cooper Institute, in New York; Packer Collegiate Institute, in Brooklyn; Rensselaer Polytechnic Institute, at Troy, New York; and Washington and Lee University, at Lexington, Virginia. He was a frequent contributor to scientific periodicals and encyclopedias; and at the time of his death was internationally famous for his research in physics.[20]

Such was the original faculty in the college. If it seems small, one must remember that the enrollment was correspondingly small and that this was only a beginning. The course of study was as broad as that in other liberal arts schools of the day and besides it had been enlarged since the University had moved to Atlanta.[21] Furthermore if a student did not want a literary education, he could enter the Law School, or the Commercial Department, which was added in 1871. (The plans for a Medical School and Engineering Department were never realized.)

The Law School was conducted by six local lawyers, who gave instruction in four departments. Judge Richard H. Clark was professor of international and constitutional law; General Lu-

20. *Who Was Who in America*, 1182; Le Conte, *Autobiography of Joseph Le Conte*, 59; Sarah Harriett Butts, ed., *The Mothers of Some Distinguished Georgians* (New York, 1912), 30.
21. Wilson, *Atlanta As It Is*, 35-37.

cius J. Gartrell, professor of criminal law; A. C. Garlington, professor of equity, jurisprudence, pleadings, and practice; Logan E. Bleckley, S. B. Hoyt, and Nathaniel J. Hammond, common law, general principles, pleadings, and practice. The law school was detached from the University and was operated at no expense to it, but was financed by the tuition fees of the students.[22]

The professors in this school were for the most part older and more experienced than the college faculty. Each had already distinguished himself at the Atlanta bar, and at least two of them, Judge Clark and General Gartrell, were well known throughout the state. A native of Georgia, but a descendant of Massachusetts Puritans, Judge Clark had served his native state in the legislature before the war. Here he made a lasting friendship with Joe Brown, who, in 1861, appointed him, with Jared Irwin and Thomas R. R. Cobb, to codify the laws of Georgia. That year he was a delegate to the secession convention and in 1862 he was made judge of the Southwestern Circuit. Equal to his love for the legal profession was his fondness for historical and genealogical research. Endowed with a retentive memory, he was an authority on the family histories of distinguished Georgians.[23]

General Gartrell had a more eventful career than Judge Clark. Educated at Randolph-Macon College in Virginia and at the University of Georgia, he was admitted to the bar in 1842 and soon entered politics. From 1847-1851 he represented Wilkes County in the legislature. In 1854 he moved to Atlanta and after only three years he was elected to Congress, was reelected in 1859, and continued until Georgia seceded from the Union. He then organized the Seventh Georgia Regiment and entered the Confederate army as a colonel. While serving at the front, he was elected to the Confederate Congress. He was loath to retire from the field, and filled only one term, after which he returned to the army and was commissioned a Brigadier General. At the end of the war he resumed his law practice in Atlanta. He was known as "the ablest criminal lawyer in the State."[24]

---

22. *Ibid.*, 35; Stacy, *Presbyterian Church in Georgia*, 128-129.
23. Thomas H. Martin, *Atlanta and Its Builders* (2 vols., Atlanta, 1902), II, 641-642.
24. *Ibid.*, 650.

A more profound legal scholar than either Judge Clark or General Gartrell was Logan E. Bleckley. Born and reared in the mountains of the extreme northeastern part of Georgia, he began the study of law at the age of eleven. Without a teacher and without the opportunity to attend college, the lad borrowed books and learned for himself. Before he was nineteen, he was admitted to the bar and for two years practiced in his native county, earning less than fifty dollars a year. In order to increase his income, he left the mountains and came to Atlanta to accept a position as bookkeeper. In 1854 he formed a law partnership with Basil H. Overby, and the firm was later joined by young John B. Gordon. By 1860 Bleckley was the most successful practitioner at the Atlanta bar. His practice was briefly interrupted by a few months' service in the Confederate army. After a medical discharge he continued his legal career.[25] His fellow lawyers described him as a man of "great intellectuality" and of "deep learning." In the courtroom he did not aim to sway the jury by emotional appeal, but his arguments were "strong, logical, impressive," and so convincing that he usually carried his point. When he taught law at Oglethorpe, he was little known outside of the city, but within twenty years he became the Chief Justice of the Supreme Court of Georgia and was recognized nationally as a jurist.[26]

The Commercial Department was formed by taking over Moore's Atlanta Actual Business College, founded in 1858 and located in downtown Atlanta on Whitehall Street at the corner of Hunter. The principal was Professor B. F. Moore, assisted by Professors J. T. Woodward and T. H. Corkill. The school aimed "to qualify young men for the duties of active business life. To accomplish this effectually," the principal advertised, "the course of studies is limited to such as are specially required for business purposes. All the teaching is therefore strictly practical, thorough, and accurate. Every student proceeds individually and independently, no classes being formed. This enables the stu-

---

25. Logan E. Bleckley, "A Letter to Posterity," *The Green Bag*, IV, 2 (1892), 49-52.
26. *A Memorial of Logan Edwin Bleckley* (Atlanta, 1907), *passim*, especially p. 28.

dent to progress without drawbacks, and to regulate his hours of recitation independently of others. Principles are thoroughly taught, and then all the multifarious operations of every kind of business are put in actual practice."[27]

The course of instruction included: Bookkeeping "in various styles and adapted to the different departments of trade"; actual business; penmanship; commercial calculations; business correspondence; and commercial law. In the bookkeeping course the student opened, wrote out, and closed "several sets of books embodying distinct features," and thus learned the subject by practice. In the actual business course actual transactions were carried on over the counter; merchandise was bought and sold; cash was received and notes given; and all the usual matters of business were illustrated and practiced. Instruction in penmanship included "both the plain and ornamental style." A booster of the business school asked, "Who does not admire the beautiful chirography to be found at Moore's Commercial College? I have a manuscript now before me, so plain and print-like that any printer who would set it up wrong ought to be condemned without benefit of clergy."[28]

A night school was opened by the University to offer the advantages of a college education to a large class who could not attend during the day. A friend of Oglethorpe explained: "Thus does this beneficent institution *popularize* a collegiate education by diffusing its blessings among the thousands of our laboring young men who have not time and means to pursue the ordinary college courses."[29] This was the first evening college in Atlanta and probably the first in the state. In establishing this department, Oglethorpe was answering a need of the new commercial and industrial South and setting an example that colleges in Georgia were slow to follow.

With so many departments and some of them off the Oglethorpe campus, college life was quite different in Atlanta from what it had been at Midway. At first classes in the college were

---

27. Wilson, *Atlanta As It Is*, 36-37.
28. *Ibid.*, 37.
29. *Ibid.*, 35.

THE ONE REMAINING DORMITORY AT OLD OGLETHORPE

originally there was no door in the center

THE JOHN NEAL HOUSE
From an old woodcut

held in temporary quarters.[30] Before removal to the "Gate City," a committee had been appointed to choose a location. The site offered on McDonough Street (the present Capitol Avenue) was considered unsuitable because it was nearly two miles from the center of town and thereby shut off from local patronage. The committee then decided to purchase the John Neal residence, one of the few fine homes spared by Sherman. The house escaped conflagration, partly because the General had made it his headquarters for awhile, and partly because burning it would have endangered the nearby Catholic property that Father O'Reilly had persuaded the Federals to save.[31]

The Neal House was conveniently situated, facing Washington Street at the corner of Mitchell and occupying the present site of the City Hall. The partitions between walls were gutted out to make class rooms, but the building was too small for a college and the yards were inadequate for a campus. Furthermore there was no dormitory space, and out-of-town students were forced to find rooms in private homes. This situation caused little inconvenience because the great majority of the college boys were from Atlanta and lived at home, walking to and fro every day. Thus the University never exercised the rigid control over students that it had maintained at Midway. But the boys thus lost many of the social contacts that are an essential part of college life.[32]

The crowded condition was increased when the University High School was established in the basement of the Neal house. Students too young or unprepared to do college work were enrolled in this school. Its faculty seem to have been as able teachers as the professors in the collegiate department. John A. Richardson, professor of mathematics, was greatly beloved. He was a handsome young man in his middle thirties, tall and commanding in person, but thoroughly genteel in manner. He had been a captain in the Confederate army and was proud of his service record.

---

30. None of the Oglethorpe records give the exact location of the temporary quarters.
31. Stacy, *Presbyterian Church in Georgia*, 129. Mr. Bell furnished some of this information.
32. Mr. Bell's information.

To secure the best from the high school boys, he appealed to their gentlemanly qualities. "He made more impression on me than any teacher I ever had," related Piromis Bell at the advanced age of ninety-three.[33] When Professor Hunter resigned to become president of the Georgia Industrial College, Professor Richardson was elected to take his place in the collegiate department of Oglethorpe.[34] He became an authority on the War Between the States. He gathered materials on the subject for nearly fifty years and published his *Defense of the South* (Atlanta) in 1914.

Professor Richardson's colleague in the high school, E. G. Moore, professor of Latin, was "a quiet, thoughtful, and dignified man and a fine Latin scholar," according to Piromis Bell. Professor Moore was a good disciplinarian, but the third member of the high school faculty, the Reverend Malcolm Janes, professor of English and Greek, kept the students terrorized. Flogging was not allowed either in the preparatory department or in the college, but Professor Janes would hit the boys on the head with a bunch of keys if he caught any one not studying. Whenever the culprit protested that he had done nothing, the crusty pedagogue would reply, "That is what I hit you for."[35]

In spite of the crowded physical handicaps of the University, every effort was made to continue the high standards maintained at Midway. Because there was not enough room for a chapel in the Neal House, compulsory attendance upon religious exercises was discontinued, but religion remained a dominant interest. Every member of the college faculty was a devout Christian, and three of them—Wills, Fraser, and Hunter—were ordained Presbyterian ministers. While the doctrines of that church were not taught,[36] the godly lives of the professors had great influence on the students. In 1872 four out of eleven graduates entered the Presbyterian ministry.[37]

The greatest single interest in the lives of the ante bellum Oglethorpe students, the literary society, was resumed as soon as the

33. Mr. Bell to the present writer.
34. Stacy, *Presbyterian Church in Georgia*, 144.
35. Mr. Bell's information.
36. Wilson, *Atlanta As It Is*, 35-36; Mr. Bell's information; *supra*.
37. Stacy, *Presbyterian Church in Georgia*, 152.

University was located in Atlanta. The Thalians and Phi Deltas
held their first meeting in November, 1870. Secrecy and rivalry
were still maintained as they formerly had been. The subjects of
discussion and debate looked more to the New South and her
problems than to slavery, secession, and states rights. In the first
anniversary after the post bellum reorganization, B. Key Thrower
was the orator for the Thalians. He chose for his subject two
lines from Longfellow's "Psalm of Life,"

> Act, act in the living present,
> Heart within and God o'erhead.

J. T. Wills (son of Dr. Wills) was the Phi Delta orator and spoke
on "The Duty of the Hour for Young Men." He concluded with
Polonius's advice to Laertes from *Hamlet*:

> This above all,—to thine own self be true;
> And it must follow, as the night the day,
> Thou canst not then be false to any man.[38]

At commencement in 1871, the president of each society had a
special function. W. A. McDowell, president of Thalia, introduced William Spencer, the orator of the society, who spoke on
"The Voyage of Life." J. H. Townsend, the head of Phi Delta,
then presented A. S. Clayton, the orator of that society, who discussed "The Spirit of the Age."[39]

This commencement, the first after Oglethorpe was removed
to Atlanta, was held during the week July 2-5 (perhaps this time
was chosen in order to avoid celebration of the "Glorious Fourth"
as in former years) and special effort was exerted to restore the
glamour and festivities of ante bellum days.[40] The Reverend
George L. Petrie, of the class of '59, gave the baccalaureate sermon, taking for his text Mark 4:28: "First the blade, then the
ear, after that the full corn in the ear." He spoke on "Progress,"
which he said was "of Divine Command." Because the University
had no chapel, the address was delivered in the First Presbyterian

---

38. *Atlanta Constitution*, Nov. 18, 1871.
39. *Ibid.*, July 4, 1871.
40. Cf. Coulter, *College Life*, 354.

Church, but as great a crowd attended as in days gone by at Midway. There were the usual Sophomore Declamation Contest, the Junior Exhibition, and besides a Freshman Declamation Contest. These were held in the auditorium of the City Hall, located diagonally across from the Neal House. Distinguished gentlemen and young ladies as well as war heroes and noted statesmen were present to hear endless hours of speaking. Though the war had noticeably changed the interests of the orators, some could not forget the recent Confederate dead. A. C. Briscoe gave a "Eulogy on General Lee," who had died the preceding October. Joseph M. Brown, son of the former governor, spoke on "Stonewall Jackson" in "an effort gemmed with poetic thought and marked beauty and force of language and imagery." The abominable practice of throwing flowers at a favorite speaker was continued. A local newspaper reported, young Brown "was deluged with boquets [*sic*], showing his popularity with the ladies."[41] There were no graduates at these exercises, but later in the year eight seniors were awarded the A.B. degree.[42]

The next year, 1872, commencement assumed the importance it had had before the war. To accommodate a larger crowd, the exercises were held in the De Give's Opera House, where the legislature held its sessions. Again to avoid celebration of the Glorious Fourth, commencement was held the first week in July. To draw a large audience, the railroads allowed half-fare rates and the crowd was the largest "since the surrender." Among the notables present were former Governor Joseph E. Brown, Mayor William Ezzard, Colonel Isaac W. Avery, Generals Albert C. Garlington, Alfred H. Colquitt, and John B. Gordon.

The last named was the principal speaker. How changed from the young man who addressed the graduating class in 1860! Dr. Wills introduced him as "the Patriot–Soldier–Orator." The General spoke on "The Defense of Truth." His speech partook of veiled references to the recent war, but he made no defense of slavery and secession. Besides this address, eight alumni of the class of '71 spoke on current topics before the M.A. degree was

41. *Atlanta Constitution*, July 6, 1871.
42. Stacy, *Presbyterian Church in Georgia*, 150.

conferred on them. The degree was no longer honorarily bestowed three years after the Bachelor of Arts to those who applied for it and were present at commencement. Henceforth they must at least make a speech.[43]

Indeed Oglethorpe was fast becoming a real University. Within two years after the removal to Atlanta, it had become an essential part of the life of the city. Its course of study was broad for that day, and its graduates were well prepared to take their places in the New South. Of the nineteen who had received their degrees in '71 and '72, five were destined to become ministers, four lawyers, two professors, and the others business men. One, Joseph M. Brown, was a future governor.

In October, 1872, Oglethorpe began its third term in the "Gate City," but hardly had it commenced when the Synod of Georgia ordered the University to be closed. The city council that had promised ten acres in addition to $40,000 changed its original agreement, omitting the offer of land. The citizens of the south side of Atlanta who had subscribed $12,000 on the condition that the University be located in their midst on McDonough Street, refused to pay when the Trustees located the University in the Neal House in the center of town. Of the remaining $28,000 subscription much was forfeited or uncollected, and what was collected was paid in small amounts at different times making investments impractical. The annual income on the endowment was estimated at $1,500 and the tuition fees at $5,000 making a total income of $6,500. But the cost of professor's salaries, interest on the unpaid balance of the Neal House, and the cost of apparatus was $17,000 per year. To meet current expenses, what was collected for an endowment was almost consumed by the fall of '72. Accordingly the Synod, finding only $2,608.88 of the entire permanent fund in the school treasury, had no other recourse but to order the closing of the institution.[44]

The seniors were given their diplomas and sorrowfully began to make plans to return to their homes. But to one graduate, at least, the closing of the University was not altogether a matter

43. *Ibid.*, July 4, 1872.
44. Stacy, *Presbyterian Church in Georgia*, 129-132.

for weeping. Immediately after receiving his diploma, William Thomas Hollingsworth was married to Mary Frances Wills, daughter of the president, who performed the ceremony at the Neal House in the presence of the seniors, the bride's family, and many friends including former Governor Brown.[45] This was the last recorded function at old Oglethorpe. The University had begun in 1835 with a prayer meeting in Milledgeville. It closed at Christmas in 1872 with a wedding in Atlanta. Perhaps this was symbolic. During all its history, religion had been the foremost interest of the faculty and most of the students. In Atlanta the University had been wedded to the ideals of the New South and was happily fulfilling the obligations of this new union.

Like Rip Van Winkle, Oglethorpe was now to sleep for forty years. The University was in a state of coma if not dead, but in 1913 Thornwell Jacobs, a grandson of one of the old professors at Midway, refounded Oglethorpe in Atlanta after he had secured adequate funds. Today the new University has a plant valued at $2,000,000 and is raising an endowment fund of $1,000,000.

By the hand of God it has risen again.

MANU DEI RESURREXIT!

---

45. *Atlanta Constitution*, Dec. 12, 1872.

Appendices

CHARTER
OF
OGLETHORPE UNIVERSITY

Whereas, the cultivation of piety and the diffusion of useful knowledge greatly tend to preserve the liberty and to advance the prosperity of a free people; and whereas, these important objects are best attained by training the minds of the rising generation in the study of useful science, and imbuing their hearts with the sentiments of religion and virtue; and whereas, it is the duty of an enlightened and patriotic legislature to authorize, protect and foster institutions established for the promotion of these important objects—

Sec. I. *Be it enacted,* That from and immediately after the passage of this act, Thomas Goulding, S. S. Davis, S. J. Cassels, S. K. Talmage, J. C. Patterson, H. S. Pratt, Robert Quarterman, Charles W. Howard, C. C. Jones, Joseph H. Lumpkin, Washington Poe, Eugenius A. Nisbet, William W. Holt, B. E. Hand, Richard K. Hines, Samuel Rockwell, John A. Cuthbert, Tomlinson Fort, J. Billups, Charles C. Mills, Charles P. Gordon, John H. Howard, Thomas B. King and Adam L. Alexander, and their successors in office, shall be, and they are hereby declared to be a body politic and corporate, by the name and style of the Trustees of the Oglethorpe University; and as such shall be capable and liable in law to sue and be sued, to plead and be impleaded; and shall be authorized to use a common seal, and to make by-laws and regulations for the government of said university, and of the Manual Labor Institute attached thereto: *Provided,* such by-laws and regulations be not repugnant to the constitution or laws of this State, or of the United States.

Sec. II. The said board of trustees shall be authorized to appoint such officers as they may think proper for their own body, and for the instruction, government management of said university, of the Manual Labor Institute attached thereto, and to remove the same from office: *Provided,* that Hopewell Presbytery, or any other assembly or body to which Hopewell Presbytery may transfer its authority over said institutions, shall have the power of confirming or annulling such appointments.

Sec. III. The said board of trustees shall have authority to confer literary degrees.

Sec. IV. The said board of trustees shall be capable of holding all manner of property, both real and personal; and shall be invested with all the rights, privileges and immunities, which now belong or appertain, or shall hereafter be granted or conveyed to said institution, or to either of them, to have and to hold the same, for the proper use and benefit of said institutions.

Sec. V. It shall not be lawful for any person to establish, keep or maintain any store or shop of any description, for vending any species of merchandise, groceries or confectionaries, of any kind whatever, within the following limits, viz. on the south side of Fishing creek, in a direction between the sites of the edifices of the said university and manual labor institute, and Milledgeville, nor within a mile and a half of the sites of either of said edifices, in any other direction. Any person violating the prohibitions contained in this section, shall be liable to be indicted as for a misdemeanor; and on conviction, shall be fined in a sum not less than five hundred dollars, nor more than one thousand dollars; the said fine to be appropriated to the benefit of said university.

Sec. VI. The term of office of the members of the said board of trustees, shall be determined and regulated, and all vacancies in any manner occurring therein, shall be filled by Hopewell Presbytery, or by such body or assembly as may receive from Hopewell Presbytery its authority over said institutions, in such manner as the body so authorized shall think proper.[1]

---

1. Prince, *Digest of the Laws of Georgia*, 1837, pp. 877-878.

ENTRANCE REQUIREMENTS

I. All examinations for admission into College shall be in the presence of the Faculty, and no person shall be admitted but by a vote taken by them for that purpose after his examination.

II. Candidates for the Freshman Class are examined in Caesar, Cicero's Select Orations, Virgil, Sallust, Greek Testament, (John's Gospel,) Graeca Minora or Greek Reader, Algebra through Equations of the First Degree, together with Latin and Greek Grammar; also, English Grammar, Geography and Arithmetic.

III. Every student, before he is admitted to an actual standing in any class, shall obtain from the Treasurer of the College, receipts by which it shall appear that he has complied with the existing orders of the Trustees in regard to expenses; which receipts he shall produce to the Officer of the College who has at that time the instruction of the class into which he desires to enter. If any officer admit a student to the recitations of his class, without receipts, such officer shall be responsible to the Treasurer for the expenses of such student; and this rule shall also be observed in regard to every student at the commencement of every College term.

IV. If any student shall be received into College after the commencement of a term, he shall pay the tuition, room-rent, &c., of the whole term.

V. No Student shall be admitted from any other College, until he produces a certificate from the proper authority, of his regular and honorable dismission and standing.[1]

---

1. T. Minutes, 1835-70, pp. 22-23.

COLLEGE LAWS

I. The hours of study shall be from the time of morning prayers till 1 o'clock, A.M., in winter, and 7 A.M., in Summer—from 9 A.M. till 12 at noon—from 2 till 5 o'clock, P.M. in winter, and 6 o'clock P.M. in summer—and from the ringing of the evening bell at night; during which time every student shall keep his room, unless called upon to recite, or unless absent by permission.

II. During the hours of relaxation no student shall go more than one mile from the College without permission.

III. When a student is absent from his recitation without the express permission of his instructor, he shall be called to account for it, and if he has not a sufficient excuse to justify his absence, he shall be reprimanded by his instructor, according to the nature of his offence, and if such absences become frequent with a student, he shall be reported to the Faculty, and be subject to such punishment as may be deemed necessary.

IV. Every student shall attend prayers in the Chapel, morning and Evening, and shall behave with gravity and reverence during the service.

V. Every student shall attend religious worship on the Sabbath, at such times and places as shall be directed, and shall be required to attend a Bible recitation on the Sabbath to be prescribed by the Faculty and shall engage in such other religious exercises as the Faculty may prescribe.

VI. Every student shall attend recitation within twenty-four hours from the time of his arrival on the College grounds.

VII. Monitors shall be appointed by the Faculty, to note down those who are absent from the religious and other exercises of the College, and report them to the Faculty.

VIII. No student shall visit or receive visits on the Sabbath, or go beyond the bounds of the College Campus, unless with express permission.

IX. Every student shall pay the utmost reverence, obedience and respect to the persons and authority of the Faculty.

X. The students shall treat each other with uniform respect and kindness.

XI. All fighting, striking, quarrelling, turbulent words or behavior, profane language, violation of the Sabbath, shall be regarded as high offences.

XII. Playing at billiards, cards or dice, or any other unlawful game, or at backgammon, or any other game for a wager, in the College is strictly forbidden.

XIII. No fire arms, sword canes, dirks, or any deadly weapon, shall be allowed to be used or kept about the College.

XIV. No intoxicating liquor shall be allowed to be brought into the College, or used by the students.

XV. No student shall keep a horse or carriage, nor shall he be allowed to hire a horse or carriage during the session, without the permission of the Faculty.

XVI. No student shall be permitted to attend any places of fashionable amusement, such as theatres, horse races or dancing assemblies during term time.

XVII. Every student during the hours of study, shall strictly abstain from hallooing, singing, loud talking, playing on a musical instrument, or other noise in College.

XVIII. Every student shall be responsible for the preservation of order in the room he occupies, unless he can make it appear he was not to blame.

XIX. The Faculty shall have authority to break open and enter any chamber at all times, when resisted; and if any student refuses to admit an officer, or to assist him suppressing any disorder when required, he shall be regarded as guilty of high offence.

XX. No combination or agreement to do any unlawful act, or to forbear compliance with any requirement of the Faculty, shall be tolerated.

XXI. The Faculty shall punish by admonition, public or private, by rustication, suspension, dismission, expulsion—or in cases where there is no prospect of reformation, and yet no flagrant crime committed, they may privately send the individual home.

XXII. As the laws are few and general, and the government designed to be that of parental authority, and as cases may occur that are not expressly forbidden by law, much is left to the discretion of the Faculty, according to the circumstance and nature of the case.

XXIII. No servant shall be employed by the students but such as the Faculty shall appoint and approve.

XXIV. No student shall be regularly discharged from College without the request or consent of his parent or guardian, made out in writing to the Faculty.[1]

---

1. T. Minutes, 1835-70, pp. 25 ff.

COURSE OF STUDY

FRESHMAN CLASS

FIRST TERM

Greek . . . . *Xenophon's Anabasis*
Latin . . . . *Cicero de Amicitia and de Senectute*
Mathematics . . . . *Algebra, (Davies' Bourdon)*

SECOND TERM

Greek . . . . *Xenophon's Cyropaedia*
Latin . . . . *Cicero de Officiis*
Mathematics . . . . *Algebra (completed)*

THIRD TERM

Greek . . . . . . *Herodotus and Thucydides, (Graeca Majora)*
Latin . . . . *Horace's Odes*
Mathematics . . . . *Geometry (Davies' Legendre)*

SOPHOMORE CLASS

FIRST TERM

Greek . . . . *Lysias and Isocrates. (Graeca Majora)*
Latin . . . . *Horace's Satires*
Mathematics . . . . *Geometry (completed)*

SECOND TERM

Greek . . . . *Demosthenes' Orations (Graeca Majora)*
Latin . . . . *Horace's Epistles and Art of Poetry*
Mathematics . . . *Davies's Plane Trigonometry and Mensuration*

THIRD TERM

Greek . . . . *Homer's Odyssey*
Latin . . . . *Livy*
Mathematics . *Davies' Spherical Trigonometry, Surveying. (begun)*
Bojeson's Roman and Grecian Antiquities,   throughout the year

JUNIOR CLASS

First Term

Greek . . . . *Plato's Crito*
Latin . . . . *Cicero de Oratore*
Mathematics . . . . . *Surveying and Navigation, (completed)*
Analytical Geometry, (begun)
Natural Philosophy . . . . *Olmsted*
Rhetoric . . . . *Blair*

Second Term

Greek . . . . *Xenophon's Memorabilia*
Latin . . . . *Cicero de Oratore*
Mathematics . . . . *Davies' Analytical Geometry*
Natural Philosophy . . . . *Olmsted*
Rhetoric . . . . *Campbell*
Logic . . . . *Hedge*

Third Term

Greek . . . . *Longimus*
Latin . . . . *Cicero de Oratore*
Mathematics . . . . . *Davies' Differential and Integral Calculus*
Botany . . . . , . . *Gray*
Evidences of Christianity . . . . *Alexander*

SENIOR CLASS

First Term

Latin . . . . *Quintilian*
Astronomy . . . . *Olmsted*
Chemistry
Moral Philosophy
Constitutional Law . . . . *Sheppard*

Second Term

Greek . . . . *Oedipus Tyrannus*
Astronomy . . . . *Olmsted*
Chemistry
Geology
Mental Philosophy

THIRD TERM

General Review

All the classes have Bible recitations every Sabbath
All the students read original essays and declaim as often as the
Faculty may direct.[1]

---

1. *Oglethorpe University Catalogue*, 1857-1858, pp. 20-22.

GRADUATES OF OGLETHORPE UNIVERSITY

Those marked with an asterisk were awarded a certificate of proficiency. All others were given a Bachelor of Arts degree.

1839

John H. Fitten
Thomas E. Lloyd

William J. Sasnett
John B. Whitehead*

1840

John Bilbo
Fleming G. Davies
William G. Davies
George W. Hardwick

Robert W. Jemison
Bedney F. McDonald
Charles S. Rockwell
Charles J. Williams

1841

Homer Hendee

Randolph Spaulding*
Charles A. Stillman

1842

James F. Bozeman
Francis T. Cullens

Theodosius Burns Davies
George W. Fish
Charles Whitmarsh Lane

1843

Abner H. Bowen
William L. Franks
James Augustine Hall
James M. King

James J. Neely
Joseph H. Nisbet*
George W. Owens
Robert A. Smith
Daniel H. B. Troup*

1844

John C. Daniel
William Ivey, Jr.
Thomas H. King
Charles E. Nisbet
James T. Nisbet
George R. Ramsay
Henry Safford, Jr.
John W. A. Sanford
James Robert Tucker

1845

Virgilius Maro Barnes
Joel C. Barnett
Groves Harrison Cartledge
Andrew J. Ford
Benjamin Fort
Moses Fort
John B. Habersham
Ellsworth T. Park
Phocion Ramsay
Elliott J. Smith
Charles E. Tefft

1846

Benjamin Leander Beall
Hines H. Goode
William Hansell Hall
Americus W. Lewis

1847

Samuel Carter*
Levi Gallimore*
Joseph S. Merrill
Joseph Melancthon Quarterman
Francis P. Stubbs
Richard Lee Warthen*
Thomas Francis Wells

1848

Benjamin F. Carter
Gurdon R. Foster
Donald Fraser
Algernon Sydney Hartridge
Lafayette Stuart Quarterman
John B. Ragland
John M. Smith
Samuel B. Spencer
Leander L. Varnedoe

1849

James H. Alexander
James S. Bivins
Charles G. Campbell
A. Walker Cassels
John Dixon Holmes
R. A. Houston

Henry Clay King
Robert W. Milner
Francis C. Morris
William H. Roane
James Stacy
William M. Tucker

Henry M. Weed

1850

Thomas J. Adams
John W. Duncan
James W. Hardee
Samuel McClary

William J. McCormick
John G. Richards
Charlton Henry Wilson
Clinton Wright

1851

Charles T. Bannerman
Andrew Bowie
Francis H. Bowman
S. A. Calhoun
Samuel Y. Carter

Samuel Hunter
John McLeod
Samuel Orr
Henry Barrington Pratt
Joseph J. West

William D. Witherspoon

1852

John E. Baker
William Henry Baker
Samuel James Bingham
William K. Blake
John Cassels
James Archibald Cousar
John Augustus Danforth

Charles H. Hall
Nathaniel Alpheus Pratt
Candor J. Silliman
Lucius A. Simonton
Arthur Melville Small
Robert Robertson Small
Thomas L. Taylor

1853

William A. Barron*
James W. Bones
James W. Boyd
James D. Clark
B. L. Cochran
William W. Cochran
Joseph L. Cunning
Thomas J. Davidson
Isaac L. Ellington*
William S. Frierson
James S. Gamble

William Hall
Emmet R. Johnson
R. A. Jones
Elmore Kinder
Andrew Rutherford Liddell
Alexander McLeod
John McLeod
John C. Moore
Walker Duncan Newell
Charles Whitfield Smith
Levi Wilcoxon

Myron D. Wood

1854

Isaac Wheeler Avery
Thomas M. Beaty
David C. Boggs
William L. Boggs
C. L. R. Boyd
M. B. Boyd
William D. Boyd
Joel C. Bristow

William T. M. Dickson
Zachariah Cox Fort
Roger L. Gamble
Andrew F. Hill
Arthur Fort Hunter
James B. Parr
Andrew Pickens Smith
William Alexander Williamson

1855

Samuel Edward Axson
Thomas Quarterman Cassels
A. M. C. Duncan
John Ferguson
Edward Ogilvie Frierson
James H. Hamilton

Holmes L. Harvey
James C. Patterson
M. M. Slaughter
Theodore E. Smith
William S. Smith
John L. Underwood

Thomas O. Wicker

1856

Robert Bradley
Elbert Calhoun
William A. Carter
B. H. Craig
H. K. Daniels

William H. Harris
Robert Warnock McCormick
William McPherson*
A. W. Millican
George S. Thomas

1857

Robert Quarterman Baker
George Scarbrough Barnsley
George A. Bivins
Frederick A. Borden
James Hamilton Bryan
George Alexander Buchanan
R. H. W. Buchanan
Samuel Jones Cassels
Warren W. W. Clay
James Smith Cozby
William T. Daniel
Robert Henry Fleming
Tomlinson Fort

D. Graham Fulton
William A. Gregg
Benjamin T. Hunter
Henry E. Martin
John B. McDowell
Duncan E. McIntyre
James M. Oliver
L. W. Philips*
Whiteford S. Ramsay
James M. Reid
William Green Robson
William E. Sherrill
Robert L. Wiggins*

Leighton B. Wilson

1858

C. B. Adams
D. S. Bethune
E. J. Bower
A. P. Calhoun
Allen Crosby
John Elbert DuBose
A. Wayne Fleming
Thomas F. Fleming
John Hardeman
Theodore Hunter
William L. Le Conte
W. Augustus Little
Daniel Milton McLure

Duncan McDuffie
Andrew W. Morrison
James Hoge Nall
Henry Sayre Orme
James A. Shingler
G. W. Smith
D. N. Speer
John F. Stinson
John M. Tarver
C. Toxey
W. S. Toxey
James F. White
Charles J. Williamson

H. Jemison Winn

1859

Caesar Augustus Baker
William B. Bingham
Samuel Dowse Bradwell
J. Douglas A. Brown
Luther Mallard Cassels
Edwin K. Fulton
Edward Melvin Green
George Francis Johnson
W. P. Johnson
Samuel Luckie Knox
George Whitfield Ladson

James W. Law
H. Stinson Little
William James Martin
A. Porteus Miller
Tomlinson Fort Newell
William Pelham
George Laurens Petrie
Samuel Henry Spencer
William W. Spencer
Frank Tufts
W. Alexander Wilson

1860

C. T. Bayne
John W. Burroughs
William Craig
W. H. Fay
Robert W. Flournoy
John Porter Fort
Joseph E. Fulton
John M. Goetchius
J. L. Greer
Thomas Hardeman

E. F. Hoge
John Q. West Kendrick
Joseph H. King
Sidney Clopton Lanier
Harrison Millican
Evan A. Presley
Nathaniel Pratt Quarterman
J. Thomas Roberts
William R. Slaughter
John Q. Spencer

1861

John W. Baker
James A. Beall
Charles M. Boyd
J. Graham Brown
Edwin Postelle Cater
James P. D. Cooper
George P. Crichton
Samuel T. Dean
John V. H. Ditmars
M. L. Frierson

John F .Green
Anthony W. Hale
John J. James
William E. James
John G. Lane
James A. McCaw
James S. McDowell
Hugh W. Montgomery
John Montgomery
Charles Phillips

Thomas J. Shine

1862

J. J. Boyd

Charles Coleman

James G. Lane

R. H. Nall

1871

Joseph Mackay Brown

B. P. Gaillard

Charles B. Gaskill

Clinton Gaskill

R. A. Massey

William Spencer

Robert Neal Smith

J. T. Wills

1872

A. C. Briscoe

W. A. McDowell

I. M. Ginn

William Thomas Hollingsworth

J. J. Johnson

John Jones

W. W. Killough

W. T. Moyers

W. A. Taylor

B. Key Thrower

Willis Venable

HONORARY DEGREES
DOCTORS OF DIVINITY

1847
Richard B. Cater

1848
Thomas Houston

1850
John Stoughton

1852
Robert H. Nall   Benjamin Morgan Palmer
John S. Wilson

1853
Carlisle Pollock Beman   E. P. Rogers

1854
Nathaniel Alpheus Pratt, Sr.

1855
Sylvester Woodbridge

1856
James C. Patterson

1857
E. T. Buist   Joseph R. Wilson

1866
J. R. Burgett   John La Fayette Girardeau
James E. Evans   David Wills

1871
R. C. McInnis   Donald McQueen

DOCTORS OF LAW

1852

William Law

1855

James Henley Thornwell, D.D.

1869

Washington Poe

1871

George Howe, D.D.   John A. Ingles

OGLETHORPE GRADUATES WHO ENTERED THE MINISTRY

1839
William J. Sasnett

1841
Homer Hendee   Charles A. Stillman

1842
Charles Whitmarsh Lane

1845
Groves Harrison Cartledge

1846
Benjamin Leander Beall   William Hansell Hall

1847
Joseph Melancthon Quarterman

1848
Gurdon R. Foster   Donald Fraser

1849
James H. Alexander   Francis C. Morris
R. A. Houston   William H. Roane
Robert W. Milner   James Stacy

1850
William J. McCormick   John G. Richards
            Charlton Henry Wilson

1851
Francis H. Bowman   Samuel Orr
            Henry Barrington Pratt

1852

Samuel James Bingham
James Archibald Cousar
John Augustus Danforth

Candor J. Silliman
Lucius A. Simonton
Arthur Melville Small

Robert Robertson Small

1853

Thomas J. Davidson
William Hall

Elmore Kinder
Andrew Rutherford Liddell

Myron D. Wood

1854

David Chalmers Boggs

William L. Boggs

Andrew Pickens Smith

1855

Samuel Edward Axson
Edward Ogilvie Frierson

Holmes L. Harvey
Theodore E. Smith

John L. Underwood

1856

Robert Bradley

William A. Carter

Robert Warnock McCormick

1857

Robert Quarterman Baker
James Smith Cozby
William A. Gregg

Benjamin T. Hunter
Duncan E. McIntyre
Whiteford S. Ramsay

Leighton B. Wilson

1858

John Elbert DuBose
Theodore Hunter

Daniel Milton McLure
Duncan McDuffie

James Hoge Nall

1859

Caesar Augustus Baker
J. Douglas A. Brown

Edward Melvin Green
George Whitfield Ladson

George Laurens Petrie

1860

W. H. Fay

Nathaniel Pratt Quarterman

1861

John V. H. Ditmars

1862

James G. Lane

R. H. Nall

1871

Robert Neal Smith

1872

I. M. Ginn
William Thomas Hollingsworth

J. J. Johnson
W. W. Killough

OGLETHORPE MATRICULATES WHO ENTERED THE MINISTRY

Benjamin Lazarus Baker

Robert Williams Bigham

William B. Crawford

Preston B. Luce

Allen T. Matthews

Le Roy P. McCutchen

Robert L. Smythe

OGLETHORPE GRADUATES WHO SERVED AS COLLEGE PRESIDENTS

John E. Baker, president of the Young Female College at Thomasville, Georgia

Samuel Dowse Bradwell, president of the State Normal School at Athens.

Homer Hendee, president of the Greensboro Synodical Female College

R. A. Houston, president of the Greensboro Synodical Female College

Benjamin T. Hunter, first president of the Georgia Industrial College at Athens

Willima J. Sasnett, president of La Grange College

Charles A. Stillman, founder and president of Stillman Institute, Tuscaloosa, Alabama

Bibliography

PRIMARY SOURCES

Manuscripts

Allen, Sarah Cantey Whitaker, "Old Oglethorpe University—Midway, Georgia." In the possession of Miss Floride Allen of Midway, Baldwin County, Ga.

Barnsley, George S., "Farewell Address to the Phi Delta Society of Oglethorpe University." In the George S. Barnsley Papers, Southern Historical Collection, University of North Carolina Library, Chapel Hill.

Barnsley, George S., "Recollections of Oglethorpe University, Midway, Ga. — 1854-1857." In the George Barnsley Papers, Southern Historical Collection.

Barnsley, George S., Letters to his father, Godfrey Barnsley. In the Godfrey Barnsley Papers, Duke University Library, Durham, N. C.

Cook, Anna Maria Green, "Diary of 1861-1867." In the possession of Mrs. Addie Cook Proctor of Midway, Baldwin County, Ga.

Charles D. Lanier Collection. In the Lanier Room, Johns Hopkins University, Baltimore, Md.

Clifford Lanier Collection. Owned by Mrs. John Tilley, Montgomery, Ala. Includes several letters of the Lanier brothers, written from Oglethorpe University, 1857, 1859-1861.

Henry W. Lanier Collection. In the Lanier Room, Johns Hopkins University, Baltimore, Md.

Pauline McKinley Collection. In the possession of Miss Pauline McKinley, Milledgeville. Includes miscellaneous letters written to Oglethorpe officials, the MS Minutes of the Executive Committee of Oglethorpe, miscellaneous newsclippings about the University, programs, and one Catalogue of Oglethorpe University, 1857-1858.

Minutes of Benevolent Lodge, No. 6, 1837-1864. These MS minutes are in the archives of the lodge in the Milledgeville Masonic Hall.

Minutes of the Executive Committee of Oglethorpe University. In the possession of Miss McKinley of Milledgeville, Ga. See supra.

Minutes of Phi Delta Literary Society, 1834-1915, of Mercer University. In the Mercer University Library, Macon, Ga.

Minutes of the Thalian Society of Oglethorpe University, 1859-1863. In the History Room of the Georgia State College for Women, Milledgeville.

Northrup Family Collection. In the Lanier Room, Johns Hopkins University.
Richards, John G., "Autobiography." In the possession of James McDowell Richards, president of Columbia Theological Seminary, Decatur, Ga.
Trustee Minutes of Oglethorpe University, 1835-1870. These MS minutes are in the vault of Oglethorpe University in Atlanta.
Trustee Minutes of Oglethorpe University, 1870-1887. These MS minutes are in the vault of Oglethorpe University in Atlanta.

PRINTED AUTOBIOGRAPHIES, LETTERS, AND REMINISCENCES OF
OGLETHORPE STUDENTS AND FACULTY

Anderson, Charles R., ed., *Sidney Lanier*. 10 vols., Centennial edition, Baltimore, 1945. Volume VII contains 16 letters written by Lanier while at Oglethorpe.
Armes, William Dallam, ed., *The Autobiography of Joseph Le Conte*. New York, 1903. Includes Le Conte's recollections of his teaching at Oglethorpe.
Bell, Piromis H., "The Calico House, " *Atlanta Historical Bulletin*, I, No. 3 (May, 1930), 28-38. An autobiographical sketch by the only living man who attended Oglethorpe.
Bleckley, Logan E., "A Letter to Posterity," *The Green Bag*, IV, No. 2 (1892), 49-52. A humorous autobiographical sketch by one of the professors of law at Oglethorpe, 1870-1872.
Cartledge, Groves Harrison, *Sermons and Discussions, with an Autobiography*. Richmond, Va., 1903. Edited by his sons, Thomas D. and Samuel J. Cartledge.
Fort, John Porter, *A Memorial and Personal Reminiscences*. New York, 1918. Includes recollections of Fort's college days at Oglethorpe.
Jacobs, Thornwell, *The Oglethorpe Story*. Atlanta, 1916. Includes recollections of several Oglethorpe alumni.
Lanier, Clifford, "Reminiscences of Sidney Lanier," *Chautauquan*, XXI (July, 1895), 403-409. Includes Clifford Lanier's recollections of his and Sidney's college days at Oglethorpe.
Lanier, Sidney, *Tiger-Lilies, A Novel*. New York, 1867. Though a novel, much of this work is obviously autobiographical and reflects the war spirit at Oglethorpe and in Georgia's capital in the winter and spring of 1861.
McAdoo, William Gibbs, *Crowded Years*. Boston and New York, 1931. An excellent autobiography by one who attended Midway Academy after the War Between the States.
Northrup, Milton H., "Recollections and Letters of Sidney Lanier," *Lippincott's Magazine*, LXXV (March, 1905), 302-15.

Richards, William C., ed., *Georgia Illustrated*. Penfield, Ga., 1842. Includes Dr. Samuel K. Talmage's "Sketch of Oglethorpe University."
Richardson, John A., *Defense of the South*. Atlanta, 1914. Partly autobiographical.
Stacy, James, *A History of the Presbyterian Church in Georgia*. n.p., 1912. Chapter VII on "Oglethorpe University" is partly autobiographical, and is the best account of the subject by an alumnus.
Varnedoe, James Oglethorpe, "Sidney Lanier: An Appreciation," *Georgia Historical Quarterly*, II (Sept., 1918), 139-44.
Woodrow, Marion W., ed., *Dr. James Woodrow: Character Sketches and Teachings*. Columbia, S. C., 1909. Includes reminiscences of several Oglethorpe alumni and of Professor Woodrow.

NEWSPAPERS AND PERIODICALS

Atlanta Constitution, Atlanta, 1870-1872, 1878.
Atlanta Weekly Intelligencer. Atlanta, 1870-1871.
Federal Union. Milledgeville, 1835-1870. The only complete file for the period is the De Renne Collection in the University of Georgia Library, Athens.
Oglethorpe University Magazine, I, 1-7 (Jan.-July, 1855). A file for this period is in the George S. Barnsley Papers, Southern Historical Collection.
Southern Recorder. Milledgeville, 1835-1870. The only complete file of this weekly for the period is in the Georgia State Library at the Capitol in Atlanta. This paper is the best single source of information on old Oglethorpe University.
Southern Presbyterian Review.

PUBLIC DOCUMENTS

Acts of the General Assembly . . . of Georgia, 1835-1872. Published separately for each session.
Candler, Allen D., editor, *The Confederate Records of the State of Georgia*. 5 vol., Atlanta, 1909-1911.
Conley, John H., *Catalogue of the Georgia State Library, 1869*. Atlanta, 1869.
Journal of the Public and Secret Proceedings of the Convention of the People of Georgia. Milledgeville, Ga., 1861.
Prince, Oliver H., compiler, *Digest of the Laws of the State of Georgia*. Second edition, Athens, 1837.

PAMPHLETS

Catalogue of the Officers and Students of Oglethorpe University, 1852-1860. Incomplete files in the De Renne Collection at the University of Georgia; in the Presbyterian archives, Montreat, N. C.; and in the Widener Memorial Library at Harvard University.

Catalogue of the Thalian Literary Society of Oglethorpe University. Charleston, S. C., 1858. In the History Room at the Georgia State College for Women, Milledgeville.

Charlton, Robert Milledge, *Address delivered before the Societies of Oglethorpe University . . . on November 16, 1842.* Milledgeville, 1842. In the De Renne Collection and in the Duke University Library.

Gordon, George A., *False Perspective. An Address before the Phi Delta and Thalian Societies of Oglethorpe University, delivered at the Commencement, on the 22nd July, 1857.* Savannah, 1857. In the De Renne Collection.

Gordon, John Brown, *Progress of Civil Liberty.* Macon, 1861. In the Georgia State Library, Atlanta.

Hamilton, William T., *Truth: its Nature and its Grandeur. An Address delivered before the Students of Oglethorpe University in the College Chapel, Sunday, September 18, 1847.* In the De Renne Collection.

Hartridge, A. Sydney, *An Oration delivered before the Phi Delta and Thalian Societies of Oglethorpe University, on the Fourth of July, 1848.* Macon, 1848. In the De Renne Collection.

Howard, Charles W., *An Appeal in Behalf of Oglethorpe University.* Augusta, 1835. In the Pauline McKinley Collection.

Johnson, Herschel Vespasian, *Obligations of Civilization to the Arts and Sciences. An Oration before the Thalian and Phi Delta Societies of Oglethorpe University. Delivered at Commencement on the 23rd of July 1856.* Milledgeville, Ga., 1856. In the De Renne Collection.

Law, Henry M., *An Address delivered before the Thalian and Phi Delta Societies of Oglethorpe University at Commencement, July 20th, 1853.* Savannah, 1853. In the De Renne Collection and in the Duke University Library.

Lumpkin, Joseph Henry, *An Address delivered before Hopewell Presbytery, the Board of Trustees of Oglethorpe University, and a Large Concourse of Ladies and Gentlemen.* Milledgeville, 1837. In the De Renne Collection.

Palmer, Benjamin Morgan, *The Claims of the English Language. An Address pronounced before Phi Delta and Thalian Societies of Oglethorpe University, Georgia on Commencement Day, November 10, 1852.* Columbia, S. C., 1853. In the De Renne Collection.

Petigru, James L., *Oration delivered before the Thalian and Phi Delta Societies of Oglethorpe University, on Commencement Day, the 10th of November, 1841.* Milledgeville, 1841. In the Rare Book Room, University of Georgia Library.

Rogers, Ebenezar Pratt, *An Oration pronounced before the Thalian and Phi Delta Societies, of Oglethorpe University, at the Annual Commencement, November 12, 1851.* Augusta, 1852. In the De Renne Collection.

Simms, William Gilmore, *Self-Development. An Oration delivered before the Literary Societies of Oglethorpe University, November 10, 1847. Published by the Thalian Society.* Milledgeville, 1847. In the De Renne Collection.

Smith, John MacNeill, *An Oration delivered before the Thalian and Phi Delta Societies of Oglethorpe University, Georgia, July 4, 1848.* Milledgeville, Ga., 1848. In the De Renne Collection.

Smyth, Thomas, *Denominational Education . . . . Address, delivered before the Thalian and Phi Delta Societies of Oglethorpe University.* Charleston, S. C., 1846. In the De Renne Collection and in the Duke University Library.

Stiles, William Henry, *Study, the Only Sure Means of Ultimate Success. An Address delivered before the Thalian and Phi Delta Societies of Oglethorpe University, Georgia at the Annual Commencement, July 19, 1854.* Milledgeville, 1854. In the De Renne Collection.

Talmage, Samuel K., *A Lecture Delivered before the Georgia Historical Society . . . on the Subject of Education.* Savannah, 1844. In the library of Columbia Theological Seminary, Decatur, Ga.

MISCELLANEOUS

Allen, Ivan, Sr., "Oglethorpe University Scrapbook." In the possession of Ivan Allen, Sr., of Atlanta. Includes valuable newsclippings.

French, Samuel G., *Two Wars: An Autobiograpy.* Nashville, 1901. Includes references to Sidney Lanier.

Le Conte, Joseph, *Evolution and Its Relation to Religious Thought.* New York, 1888.

Le Conte, Joseph, *Religion and Science.* New York, 1877.

Massey, Kate, "A Picture of Atlanta in the Late Sixties," *Atlanta Historical Bulletin,* V (Jan., 1940), 32-36.

Personal Memoirs of Gen. W. T. Sherman [*by Himself*]. 2 vols., New York, 1890. Volume II includes references to Milledgeville during the famous March through Georgia.

SECONDARY SOURCES

Alderman, Edwin A., and Joel Chandler Harris, eds., *Library of Southern Literature.* 17 vols., Atlanta, 1907-1923. Includes biographical sketches of Oglethorpe students and faculty, together with selections from their writings.

American Almanac and Repository of Useful Information, 1830-1861. Boston. Published yearly.

Avery, Isaac W., *The History of the State of Georgia, from 1850 to 1881.* New York, 1881.

Baker, Ray Stannard, *Woodrow Wilson: Life and Letters.* 8 vols., New York, 1927-1935. Volume I includes biographical sketches of Professor James Woodrow and Dr. Joseph R. Wilson, a trustee of Oglethorpe.

Baskervill, William M., *Southern Writers: Biographical and Critical Studies.* 2 vols., Nashville, 1899.

Beeson, Leola Selman, *Sidney Lanier at Oglethorpe.* Macon, 1936.

Butts, Sarah Harriett, comp., *The Mothers of Some Distinguished Georgians.* New York, 1912. Includes biographical sketches of the mothers of Oglethorpe men.

Clay, Hiland H., *Genealogy and History of the Clay Family,* n.p., 1916.

Cleveland, Henry, *Alexander H. Stephens, in Public and Private with Letters and Speeches, before, during, and since the War.* Philadelphia, 1866.

Cook, Anna Maria Green, *History of Baldwin County, Georgia.* Anderson, S. C., 1925.

Cooper, Walter G., *Official History of Fulton County.* Atlanta, 1934.

Coulter, E. Merton, *College Life in the Old South.* New York, 1928. An excellent study of college life at the University of Georgia prior to 1870.

Coulter, E. Merton, *Georgia: A Short History.* Chapel Hill, N. C., 1947.

Entered into Rest June 13, 1896, Rev. Charles Whitmarsh Lane, D. D. Athens, Ga., n. d. A pamphlet in the Lanier Room of Thalian Hall, Midway, Ga.

Flippin, Percy Scott, *Herschel V. Johnson of Georgia, State Rights Unionist.* Richmond, Va., 1931.

Godbold, Albea, *The Church College of the Old South.* Durham, N. C., 1944.

Graham, Philip Edwin, "James Woodrow, Calvinist and Evolutionist," *Sewanee Review*, XL (July-Sept., 1932), 307-15.

History of the Baptist Denomination in Georgia, with Biographical Compendium. Atlanta, 1881. Contains a biographical sketch of Professor N. M. Crawford.

Hull, Augustus L., *Annals of Athens, Georgia, 1801-1901.* Athens, 1906.

Hull, Augustus L., *A Historical Sketch of the University of Georgia.* Atlanta, 1894.

Jacobs, Thornwell, ed., *William Plumer Jacobs, Literary and Biographical.* Oglethorpe University, Ga., 1942.

Johnson, Allen, and Dumas Malone, eds., *Dictionary of American Biography.* 20 vols., index, and supplements. New York, 1928-

Johnston, Richard Malcolm, and William Hand Browne, *Life of Alexander H. Stephens.* Philadelphia, 1883.

Jones, Charles E., *Education in Georgia.* Washington, 1889.

Jones, F. D., and W. H. Mills, *History of the Presbyterian Church in South Carolina since 1850.* Columbia, S. C., 1926.

Knight, Lucian Lamar, *Georgia's Landmarks, Memorials and Legends.* 2 vols., Atlanta, 1913-1914.

Knight, Lucian Lamar, *Reminiscences of Famous Georgians.* 2 vols., Atlanta, 1907. Includes biographical sketches of Oglethorpe students and faculty.

LaMotte, Louis C., *Colored Light: The Story of the Influence of Columbia Theological Seminary, 1828-1937.* Richmond, Va., 1937.

Lanier, Henry W., ed., *Selections from Sidney Lanier, Prose and Verse.* New York, Chicago, and Boston, 1916.

Lorenz, Lincoln, *The Life of Sidney Lanier.* New York, 1935. Includes bits of information on Lanier's college days not found elsewhere.

Martin, Thomas H., *Atlanta and Its Builders.* 2 vols., Atlanta, 1902. Includes biographical sketches of Oglethorpe professors who taught in the University after it removed to Atlanta.

A Memorial of Logan Edwin Bleckley. Atlanta, 1907.

Memorial Volume of the Semi-Centennial of the Theological Seminary at Columbia, South Carolina. Columbia, 1884. Includes biographical sketches of Oglethorpe alumni who attended Columbia Theological Seminary.

Mims, Edwin, *Sidney Lanier.* Boston and New York, 1905. An excellent biography of Sidney Lanier, with good information on college days at Oglethorpe.

The National Cyclopedia of American Biography. 35 vols., and supplement, 1891-

Northen, William J., ed., *Men of Mark in Georgia*. 7 vols., Atlanta, 1906-1912.

Orr, Dorothy, *A History of Education in Georgia*. Chapel Hill, 1950. Includes a biographical sketch of Professor Gustavus J. Orr.

Phillips, Ulrich B., *The Life of Robert Toombs*. New York, 1913.

Sherwood, Adiel, *A Gazetteer of Georgia*. Macon, Griffin, and Atlanta, 1860. Includes a sketch of Oglethorpe University in 1860.

Snyder, Henry Nelson, *Modern Poets and Christian Teaching: Sidney Lanier*. Cincinnati, 1906.

Stacy, James, *History of Midway Congregational Church, Liberty County, Georgia*. Newnan, Ga., 1899. Includes biographical sketches of Oglethorpe students and faculty who were members of Midway Church.

Starke, Aubrey Harrison, *Sidney Lanier: A Biographical and Critical Study*. Chapel Hill, N. C., 1933. The best biography of Lanier, with helpful information on his college days and tutorship at Oglethorpe.

White, George, *Historical Collections of Georgia*. New York, 1854.

White, Georgia, *Statistics of the State of Georgia: including an account of its Natural, Civil, and Ecclesiastical History; together with a Particular Description of each County, Notices of the Manners and Customs of its oboriginal Tribes, and a correct map of the State*. Savannah, 1849.

Who's Who in America. Chicago, 1899-   . Published biennially.

Who Was Who in America, 1897-1942. Vol. I, Chicago, 1942. Only one volume published.

Williams, Eleanor, *Ivan Allen, A Resourceful Citizen*. Atlanta, 1950.

Wilson, John S., *The Dead of the Synod of Georgia: Necrology, or Memorials of Deceased Ministers*. Atlanta, 1869. Includes biographical sketches of Dr. Samuel K. Talmage, and of several Oglethorpe alumni.

Wilson, John Stainback, *Atlanta As It Is*. New York, 1871. Includes the best sketch of Oglethorpe University after it removed to Atlanta in 1870.

Index

Unless otherwise indicated
all references pertain to Oglethorpe University
Graduates of Oglethorpe are listed
in Appendix, *supra*, 156-161

Printed in the United States
154424LV00001B/69/P